Dories, Ho!

Matt and Karen Smith

To see color versions of the photos in this book and additional photos from our trip, visit our website:

www.doriesho.com

ISBN-10: 1977717845 (paperback)
ISBN-13: 9781977717849 (paperback)

Disclaimer: This book reflects the opinions of the authors related to their experiences while traveling. Details of certain events may have been edited for stylistic considerations.

Front cover photo: Lolly Anderson

"The best way for people to understand how important it is to have the bottom of the Grand Canyon preserved, and have its aquatic life saved, and its riparian zone with the beauty that's there, kept, is perhaps to have them on that river and let them feel the way it stirs and rumbles and moves you along at its own pace, and to sense the kind of 'life' the river has. It has a tremendous force and appeal that I can't describe."*

Martin Litton

*Articulate Outrage, Righteous Wrath—Martin Litton. *boatman's quarterly review*, *Volume 28 number 1*(winter 2014-2015), page 35.

Matt and Karen Smith on the Colorado River
in Grand Canyon National Park, September 2016

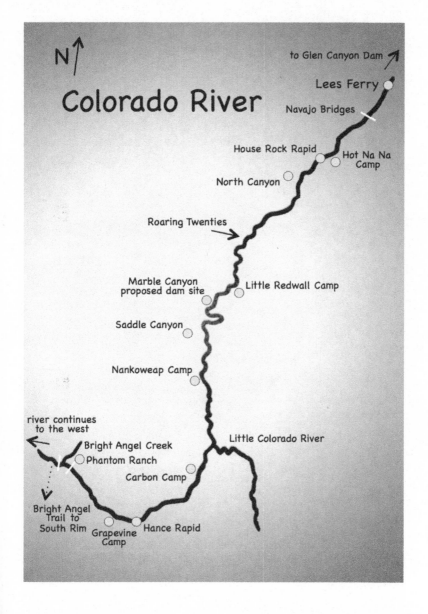

N

Colorado River

to Glen Canyon Dam

Lees Ferry

Navajo Bridges

House Rock Rapid

Hot Na Na Camp

North Canyon

Roaring Twenties

Marble Canyon proposed dam site

Little Redwall Camp

Saddle Canyon

Nankoweap Camp

river continues to the west

Bright Angel Creek

Phantom Ranch

Carbon Camp

Little Colorado River

Bright Angel Trail to South Rim

Grapevine Camp

Hance Rapid

SEPTEMBER 27
HANCE RAPID, COLORADO RIVER

Rondo guided the dory to the exact spot where he wanted to enter the rapid. When we reached a point about fifty feet from the top of the hole, the river took control. It was the point of no return, and all of us, Rondo included, were just holding on for dear life. The power of the river's current was impressive. Our speed accelerated gradually at first, and then picked up quickly until it felt like we went into a free fall. The fall ended with a bang at the bottom of the hole. The river tossed the dory in all directions. Rondo paddled furiously, and within seconds we were on the duck pond. "Bail!" he yelled.

I reached for my bailing jug and smacked heads with Iain. He was bailing like a mad man. His scoops were so fast I couldn't time mine to keep from banging into him. I lifted my legs and put them on the deck in front of us to stay out of his way. He had the footwell cleared in no time. "Good job!" yelled Rondo, "It's not over yet, hold on!"

The water rodeo resumed. I still couldn't tell where the tongue was, but Rondo seemed to have the boat right where he wanted it. He was making big, lunging paddles between waves. He hollered in our direction, "I need you to lean into that last big wave. I'll tell you when."

By then, Iain and I had gotten the hang of high siding; we were ready. Our dory passed through a couple of large waves head on. The third wave was the biggest. Rondo shouted, "This is it!" That's all he needed to say. Iain and I stood up and pushed all of our weight onto the front deck of the boat as it hit the wave and went vertical. Water came over the bow and drenched us, but the mass of our bodies was enough to keep the dory from flipping backward. Once we reached the back side of the wave, I heard shrieks and peals of laughter from Karen and Gill as the stern lifted high out of the water. What a thrill! We made it through Hance Rapid right side up.

It was over as fast as it had started. We were back on flat water peacefully floating downstream. Rondo turned the *Shoshone* 90 degrees so we had a good view of the boats behind us navigating the rapid we'd just come through. As I watched, I could see all of the passengers laughing uncontrollably as the river tossed them about. It *was* turning into the best trip of all time.

BUCKET LIST

I had wanted to float the Colorado River through the Grand Canyon for a long time. Countless people told me over the years that it had been their favorite trip, ever. Regardless of their age or how much they'd traveled otherwise, their descriptions were always similar, "Best trip of all time!" I asked Karen if she would be up for spending a week or two on a small boat at the bottom of the Grand Canyon and camping on sandy riverbanks.

"Yes! That's in my bucket!" she said.

"What? What's in your bucket?" I asked.

"A Grand Canyon river trip. It's in my bucket."

"What bucket are you talking about?'

"My bucket of wishes! It's on my bucket list."

"Sweetie, what do you think the term 'bucket list' means?"

"It's the list of wishes that are in your bucket."

"Please tell me you don't have a real bucket somewhere with wishes in it."

She frowned at me. "It's not a real bucket, Matt; it's a figure of speech."

"OK, that's not what bucket list means."

"Of course it is. What do you think it means?"

"It's the list of things you want to do before you kick the bucket—before you die."

Karen put her thumb and index finger together and pressed them to her lips. This is what she does when she thinks, "Oh shit, maybe he's right." She squinted her eyes and didn't respond for a long time.

Then, she said abruptly, "No. It's the list of wishes in your wish bucket. Haven't you heard of the phrase, 'pocket full of wishes'?"

"Then why isn't it called a pocket list?" I asked.

"Because pocket list sounds stupid," she replied.

"I want to make sure I have this correct. You have an imaginary bucket into which you've placed imaginary pieces of paper. On each imaginary piece of paper, you've written a wish. And this, this is your bucket list. Did I get that right?"

There was another long, squinting pause.

"Are you sure about kicking the bucket? That doesn't seem right to me."

"Look it up, and we'll see," I replied.

Karen's exhaustive Internet search about the origins of the term "bucket list" did not produce a single mention of wish buckets, so she concluded, "OK, well, we're both right."

That settled it. We were both right. Yet the river trip wish sat in her bucket for years, lonely and waiting. Then, when we were on a hiking trip with our close friends, Craig and Aya (also from the Seattle area), the topic of floating the Colorado River through the Grand Canyon came up. They were even more excited about the idea than we were. "What are we waiting for?" Craig asked. "There will never be a better time to go than now."

"Let's do it," they both said.

"We're in!" was our enthusiastic reply.

Fully expecting another couple of years to go by before the topic re-emerged, I was surprised a week later when Craig called me to discuss potential dates for a dory trip. "Next year is sold out, so we're looking at two years from now," he said. "We need to submit a request for a couple of dates and tell them the number of people in our group. The guide company will then sort through all of their early requests and let us know if we got one of our choices. Each trip has room for sixteen. How many spaces should we request?"

"All of them," I replied.

"All sixteen? You think we can fill up an entire trip?"

"Of course we can. No problem," I confidently replied.

In the ten seconds that it took me to respond, I had unthinkingly committed to a sizable financial obligation without any idea of whether we could find twelve more people to join us on the trip. We had to narrow our list of friends to those who were hearty enough to rough it outside for a week, adventurous enough to enjoy the white water rapids, and physically fit enough to do the strenuous ten-mile hike out of the canyon at the end of the trip. As it turned out, finding enough friends who wanted to do it as much as we did was the easy part. Craig and Aya invited three couples, we invited three couples, and they all said, "Yes," immediately. As one of the wives put it, "It's going to be epic!" I didn't understand what she meant by "epic," but I agreed and then awkwardly high-fived her fist bump.

This is the story of our adventure floating the Colorado River from Lees Ferry to Phantom Ranch: a journey of six days with fourteen friends, ten crewmembers, four dories, three supply rafts, and one magnificent Grand Canyon.

DORIES, HO!

Karen and I married in the early '80s (the *nineteen* eighties that is). Since then, we've managed to give life to three other humans who've now moved out of our home, secured employment (including health insurance), and no longer require our daily attention. We reached this milestone of independence several years before our Grand Canyon river trip and since then have spent much of our time traveling to amazing outdoor places in the United States. Many of our destinations have been national parks, as is the Grand Canyon. In fact, there was a stretch when we visited so many of the parks in such a short period of time that we decided to slow down, catch our breath and revisit many of these locations so we could experience them more deeply, and at a slower pace.

Dories, Ho! is not the first book we've written about our travel experiences. We also wrote and published *Dear Bob and Sue*, a book about our travels to the national parks. We formatted *Dear Bob and Sue* as a series of emails to our friends Bob and Sue who couldn't join us on our trip. Karen wrote some of the emails as did I, and they were all labeled so the reader would know who authored each. *Dories, Ho!* has a more traditional format with a single author's voice throughout: mine. Yet, we've listed both of us as authors.

While I did much of the writing, Karen's input was critical. She was more than an editor; we were co-authors.

She also came up with the title. Of the roughly 80,000 words that it took to compose this book, few are more critical to its commercial success than the ones that make up the title. As with all editorial decisions, Karen and I have an equal say, and we verbally arm wrestle over each one until we happily agree. "Let's see a smile," is how many of these discussions end.

Karen was proud of her title suggestion; I wanted to call the book *Dear Bob and Sue Two*. Since this book is titled *Dories, Ho!* you know who won that argument.

"I'm not wild about the title *Dories, Ho!*," I told Karen after she suggested it.

"What's wrong with *Dories, Ho!*?" she asked.

"I'm worried people won't know what it means."

"That's not necessarily a bad thing. It'll make readers curious. It stands out."

"Or, the title might be so confusing that they don't want to read the book. Plus, I don't like the word 'ho' in the title. It sounds too much like Doris Ho. People might think it's a book about a prostitute named Doris."

"It's Dories, not Doris!"

"I get that. My point is, when people first read the title they might be confused. Do most people know what a dory is?" I thought, "They probably know what a ho is."

Karen responded, "Of course they do." Although, I heard hesitation in her voice.

"Did *you* know what a dory was before we signed up for this trip?" I asked her.

"They don't have to know what a dory is; they can Google it."

"You want to give our book a title that confuses people, so they're enticed to read it, but before they start reading the book with a confusing title, they have homework. *This* is your marketing plan?"

"Yes, that's exactly right."

And so, our book is titled *Dories, Ho!*

To all of you who've made it past the confusing title and have read this far in the book, thank you. As for the homework, I'll save you a few clicks with a cut and paste from Wikipedia: "The dory is a small, shallow-draft boat, about 16 to 23 feet long. It is usually a lightweight boat with high sides, a flat bottom and sharp bows."

Remember, it's "dories" not "Doris," and I'll explain the "Ho!" part later.

BOOKING THE TRIP

Had Craig not taken charge and presented us with a simple yes-no decision we might still be trying to decide which river trip to take. I can think of at least five things to consider when choosing a Grand Canyon river trip: cost, type of boat, which guide company to go with, route and time of year.

On top of those factors, there is also the decision whether to take a commercial trip, or if you are an experienced boater, enter the lottery for a chance to do a private trip. Even though there were boaters in our group, we never entertained the idea of attempting a private trip. The fact that you are reading this book is proof that we went with a guide company. Had we chosen to float the Colorado River through the Grand Canyon on our own, without a guide, I have no doubt someone would have written an entirely different book about our adventure. Possibly with a title such as *The Smith Party: One man's story of survival in the wilderness.*

The promotional excerpt might read: *Two days after the group began their trip, a park ranger found Smith naked and shivering a mere five miles downstream from Lees Ferry. All he was wearing was a yellow safety helmet with the word "Captain" written in black marker over every square inch. Smith was clutching a half-used roll of toilet paper. When the ranger tried to take it from him, he became very agitated and yelled, "The key! The key! Don't lose the key!" With some difficulty, rescuers loaded him into a life flight helicopter while Smith whispered in a hoarse voice, "Sand, everywhere."*

There was no sign of the other fifteen members of the party. They vanished without a trace. The only evidence of their survival comes in the form of a poor quality video that appeared on the Internet of a group that looks similar to the lost rafters. It shows them huddled together with their arms around each other crying, or possibly laughing, it's hard to tell. They appear to be drinking from liquor bottles. One of the figures has the words "captain this" written in marker across his bare chest.

While Karen Smith, wife of the rescued survivor, cannot be seen clearly in the video, a Smith family member is certain that the blurry figure in one of the scenes is her doing what they called the "Pee Wee Herman tequila dance." The group can be heard at the end of the video chanting, "Diablo Mateo no mas, Diablo Mateo no mas." No one has been able to make sense of these random, meaningless details. We may never know the whereabouts of the missing rafters.

No, we did not consider a private trip.

Going with a commercial outfit is not inexpensive. Costs vary depending on the type of trip, length, the number of days, etc. For us, this was a once in a lifetime event. Was it worth it? In my opinion, yes, it was worth every cent. Given the time, effort and supplies that go into putting on a trip like this, I understand why the guide companies have to charge the prices they do to have a viable business.

Current float trip rates are easily accessed on the Internet or directly from the guide companies. You can find a list of commercial river trip concessionaires on the Grand Canyon National Park website.

One detail that made it much easier for us to choose which guide company to go with was our choice of boat type. Maybe it was because we all had just read *The Emerald Mile* or because Craig did the research and made the decision for us, not sure which, but dories it was. (*The Emerald Mile* is a bestselling book by Kevin Fedarko about a record setting dory trip through the Grand Canyon that took place in 1983 during a rare flow surge of the Colorado River.) When doing his research, Craig read a comparison between riding in a motorized raft versus a dory. The article likened the motorized raft to riding in a car and the dory to riding a bike.

Once we decided to go with dories, there were only a couple of companies listed on the Grand Canyon National Park website that offered dory trips. The company we chose was O.A.R.S. They provided our group with an incredible experience.

I thoroughly enjoyed riding in the dories, but I'm curious what it would have been like to float the Colorado River on the other boat types. Rafts are by far more prevalent than dories. Out of the sixteen guide companies who offer river trips through the Grand Canyon, most of them offer trips using rafts as their main boat type.

Paddle rafts are the smallest type of raft. On a paddle raft trip, passengers are required to paddle the entire way. There are also oar raft trips. Typically on an oar raft trip, passengers ride while a boatman or boatwoman rows. There are also hybrid raft trips on which there is a combination of oar and paddle rafts. On a hybrid trip, passengers typically have a chance to experience both types of rafts during the course of the trip. Some companies also offer inflatable kayaks as an option, usually in conjunction with a paddle raft trip.

Based on numbers of passengers per year, motorized raft trips are the most popular. They're the largest boat type on the river, move fastest through the canyon, and are also less likely to flip. It is however, possible for *every* boat type to flip. Regardless of which watercraft you are in, the conditions and outcomes can be unpredictable. That's part of the deal.

The route we chose was Lees Ferry to Phantom Ranch. With Lees Ferry being the beginning, Phantom Ranch (between mile 88 and 89) is the mid-point on river trips through the Grand Canyon, but it isn't halfway. It's the middle because it's the only practical place for people to hike out when they're only going part of the way through the canyon, or to hike in if they're joining a trip for the last portion. Pearce Ferry, a popular take out spot for trips going the entire length of the canyon is just outside the boundaries of the park at mile 280, but many river trips cover less than 280 miles.

O.A.R.S. sent us the itinerary well in advance of the trip: meet the lead boatman at the DoubleTree Hotel in Flagstaff the night before we launch; next day go by van to Lees Ferry; spend six days on the river; stay overnight at Phantom Ranch (at the bottom of the canyon); hike the next day from Phantom Ranch to the South Rim along the Bright Angel Trail; and from there take a shuttle back to the DoubleTree Hotel in Flagstaff.

Other routes that are typically offered by river guide companies are Lees Ferry to Diamond Creek (225 miles), Lees Ferry to Pearce Ferry (280 miles), Phantom Ranch to Whitmore Wash (100 miles), and Whitmore Wash to Pearce Ferry (92 miles). There may be other routes available, but these are the most popular. Not all of these routes are offered with each boat type or every time of year.

The National Park Service limits the size of any group to twenty-six people. This limit includes passengers and staff. Our trip had sixteen paid passengers and ten staff including the boatmen. Not all trips have twenty-six people.

If all of these options are not enough, there is one more factor to consider: what time of year to go. When we booked our trip, O.A.R.S. offered dory trips from April through October. We wanted to go late enough in the year so that it wouldn't be too hot, yet not so late that it might be cold. We also learned that the National Park Service does not allow motor-powered watercraft on the river after September 15th. With this restriction, the river is less crowded after the 15th— and less noisy. All considered, the last week in September was one of our choices and we were fortunate to get it.

Of all the options we chose, there is only one thing I would have done differently with the benefit of hindsight: we should have floated the entire length of the canyon rather than only the first half. When it came time to disembark at Phantom Ranch, no one was ready to leave.

A REASON TO SHOP

From Karen's perspective, one advantage of booking a trip two years in advance is it gave her an excuse to shop. I'm sorry, I should say it gave her *another* excuse to shop. As soon as we received our confirmation from O.A.R.S., she found the suggested packing list on their website and began searching for things she needed.

There is a distinct pattern to Karen's shopping. It begins with an exhaustive Internet search. For days, whenever I walk past her while she's using her laptop, I see pages of models scrolling down her screen as she flicks her fingers across the trackpad. I don't remember ever seeing her stop and look at any individual items; they just keep scrolling by at a constant rate. There are times I'm sure she's hypnotized herself. Now and then she interrupts the scrolling with a burst of keystrokes. Days later, UPS, FedEx, and the United States Postal Service take turns pulling into our driveway to unload their trucks at our front door. I have no doubt Amazon has our house on a map somewhere as a beta test site for drone delivery in the future.

Once the heap of new clothing candidates gets so large that I can no longer see the chair in the corner of our bedroom onto which Karen has piled them, it's time for what I call "fashion show." Fashion show is when Karen tries on each outfit, looks at herself from every angle in the mirror while wearing it, and then comes out of the closet and asks me if I like it. Sometimes she waits for my response, and sometimes she disappears before I look up from what I'm doing.

In all the years we've been married, I can't remember disliking a single piece of clothing or accessory Karen has modeled for me. She'll say this isn't true. She loves to tell a story about when we were first married, and she tried on a long, form-fitting brown dress. The story ends with a theatrical finish, "I asked him if he liked my new dress and, and, and, he said I looked like a sausage!" With open mouth looks of shock, the person to whom she's told the story invariably turns to me and says, "Why would you ever say that to your lovely wife?" No one wants to hear my side of the story, which is—I like sausage! There are few things I hold in higher regard than sausage. *If* this story happened the way Karen tells it, which I'm not confirming it did, I still say my record of liking every outfit she's modeled for me is intact.

Nearly as bad was the time, more recently, when she modeled a new dress for me that she had planned on wearing to a friend's wedding. I was tired and distracted, and without thinking, I told her she looked nice. I knew as soon as I said the words that it was a mistake. Apparently telling my wife she looks nice in a dress is almost as bad as saying she looks like a sausage.

"*Nice?* Your grandmother looks nice," she said.

"I meant to say you look *really* nice. How's that?"

"Women don't want their husbands to think they look nice; they want their husbands to think they look *hot*."

"Got it."

One evening I was sitting on our bed responding to email. The door to our closet was closed, but I could hear what sounded like fashion show going on behind the door. Karen came out and said, "What do you think?"

"What do I think about what?"

"It's fashion show! What do you think?"

"I like it! That shirt will be perfect for hiking in the canyon."

"I've had this shirt for five years. I meant what do you think about the shorts?"

"They're hot. I mean they look hot. No, *you* look hot. You look hot in those shorts. That's what I meant."

There was a long pause, which I interpreted as her allowing me a moment to reconsider my answer. Either that or she was trying to figure out how to bury my body in the crawl space of our house without anyone knowing, or losing her spot on the river trip.

"I like them. I do. But, and I still like those new, hot shorts, but don't you already have a million pairs of hiking shorts?"

"*No*, and even if I did, I need a new pair for the hike out of the Grand Canyon."

"What about the pair you wore the last time we hiked to Phantom Ranch?"

"I can't wear those. People will see me in photos of both hikes and think that I've worn the same hiking shorts for the last four years."

She had a point. Earlier we'd been looking at the pictures we took years ago in front of each park sign when we visited all fifty-nine national parks. We are still wearing the same hiking clothes that we were wearing in those photos. When I looked further back in our photo collection, I realized we've been wearing mostly the same outdoor travel clothes for the past ten years. Although it felt a little bit like rolling a snowball off the top of a snowy peak, I said to her, "Yeah, maybe it would be a good idea to get some new clothes for the trip."

"What about you? Do you know what you need for the trip?"

"Don't worry about me. I have my master list."

"Well, you better look at O.A.R.S' suggestions. There are things they recommend that I know you don't have on your *master list*, like a sarong."

"Did you say, 'sarong'?"

"Yes, a sarong. You wear it loosely around your body so you can change your clothes discretely when other people are around."

"That's not a guy thing. I don't need a sarong."

"Guys use them. I read a travel blog post that said men wear them to change, you know, their shorts."

"Maybe you think you read that, but I'm sure only women wear sarongs. And if I'm wrong, I'm still not wearing a sarong, *ever*."

"Then how are you going to change your clothes without people seeing you naked?"

"Not with a sarong."

"Seriously."

"I'll wait until everyone's heads are turned or go behind a bush. I don't know."

"You can't wait until everyone turns their heads. There will be like twenty-five people on our trip."

"Don't worry; I'll figure it out. A sarong? I think you are making this up."

I never got a sarong, and neither did Karen. She was correct, though. Early one morning on the river I saw one of the boatmen getting ready for the day. He stood up in the center of his dory and put a sarong on over his board shorts. It was apparent he'd done this many times before because he slipped out of his old shorts and into new ones effortlessly. And most importantly, without me seeing anything that I wish I hadn't.

With a weight and volume limit on the personal items we could bring, we had to choose our shoes carefully. We would be standing in water, going on hikes during the heat of the day, and hiking out of the canyon at the end of the week. It would have been nice to have different footwear for each of those activities and a dry pair at night when it got cooler, but we didn't have the luxury of taking that many pairs. In the end, I took three pairs of shoes on the trip: a set of flip flops, a very light pair of running shoes, and a pair of water shoes. The water shoes were also suitable for hiking; they had closed toes and webbing that came over the top of my feet. Those three were the right combination for me. Karen brought very similar shoes, but it took a long time—like two years—for her to make her final selections.

In that time, I saw three different pairs of water shoes come and go. I don't know where they went. I suspect Karen donated them to Goodwill. I'm pretty sure she later went back to the Goodwill store and re-bought one of the pairs she had donated.

Every time a new pair would arrive at our front door I would brace for the same conversation.

"Do you like this color?" The conversation always began with the color.

"Yes, but I don't think color is the most important feature you should be concerned about."

"I like green, but not mossy green. Not for water shoes. They should be more of a forest green."

Karen often makes comments to me in which there is no question, yet the expression on her face afterward suggests she expects an answer. Gals, I think I speak for most guys when I say, "This is confusing." When Karen does this, I look back at her with an expression that says, "Was there anything else you wanted to say?"

"So, do you like this color?" she asked.

"Um, same answer as thirty seconds ago, yes."

"Not too mossy green?"

"No, not *too* mossy green. They are just the right amount of mossy green."

"I don't want mossy green." Again I get the look that suggests I should answer a question that wasn't asked.

"Alright, I don't even know what mossy green is. I'm going back to my original answer that I like the color, which, by the way, is not the most important feature you should be concerned with when it comes to shoes that will be attached to your feet for sixteen hours a day."

"Well, they need to look good."

"Regardless of what color they are now, they'll be brown by the end of our first day on the river. If I were you, I would make sure they're comfortable and broken in by the time we start the trip."

Another item Karen needed was a headlamp. Twice a week for nearly two years, she would say to me, "I need to get a headlamp for the trip." I didn't understand why she kept telling me this until I realized what she meant to say all those times was, "*You* need to buy me a headlamp for the trip." For an unknown reason, she designated me the headlamp expert in our household. I don't even know what a lumen is. I certainly don't know what eighty lumens means. And there is a wide price range on these things. I was OK with putting "headlamps" on my list of items to get for the trip, mainly because it gave me the chance to buy gadgets without Karen asking me over and over why I thought I needed them.

It took several visits to the local REI to inspect every headlamp they sell. I had to try each of them on, and then turn the light on and walk through the store looking for Karen to embarrass her. I never became convinced that one was better than the other, except when it came to lumens; the more lumens, the better. Finally, I just bought Karen the one that was on sale. I didn't buy the same model for myself. Home Depot sold a headlamp that was a little bulkier than the ones at REI, but much less expensive.

When I brought Karen's headlamp home, I was expecting an enthusiastic response. All she said was, "Thanks. Can you put it over there on my pile of stuff for the trip?" For a few weeks, I prodded her to open the box and try it on, but she wouldn't. Then finally, *I* opened the box, put in the batteries and made her try it on. I didn't want her to wait to test it for the first time the night before the trip and find out there was something wrong with it, or it didn't fit.

Karen placed it on her head, and with a few adjustments, it fit just right. By clicking the button on the front, she cycled through the three levels of brightness. With the headlamp still lit and strapped to her head, she turned away from me and walked across the room. It was then that I saw there was a red blinking light on the battery pack attached to the strap at the back of her head. I hadn't realized until then that I'd bought her a headlamp made for biking. It wasn't a big deal, but I didn't tell her because I knew she would want me to return it — and I had already checked "headlamps" off my list.

Karen didn't know until I wrote the first draft of this book why I called her "blinky" at night on the river.

GETTING INTO SHAPE

Despite being in reasonably good hiking shape, the thought of having to climb out of the Grand Canyon made us wonder if we could do it without significant difficulty when the time came. Never mind that the hike was nearly two years away. It doesn't take long to lose your physical fitness, so we made sure we always had a strenuous hike or two planned for the upcoming months to keep us from falling back into what Bill Bryson once described as "waddlesome sloth."

One thing we had going for us was that we'd hiked the Bright Angel Trail from Phantom Ranch to the South Rim in June four years earlier. We were familiar with the trail, and remembered having some difficulty on the last mile or so of the hike out. Karen and I had hiked down the day before and spent the night in one of the Phantom Ranch cabins (something we highly recommend to anyone fortunate enough to get a reservation). The next morning we left at 5:00 am to hike back to the rim of the canyon. Because of our early departure, we skipped our morning coffee. The combination of a strenuous hike, full-on summer sun, temps in the 90s, and no caffeine gave me a splitting headache that morning. Being that we'd booked our river trip for late September, I was hopeful that the temperature would be cooler on our next hike up Bright Angel Trail.

The itinerary O.A.R.S. sent us contained a lot of helpful information and emphasized the difficulty of the hike out of the canyon. It stressed the importance of being physically fit. "The hike from Phantom Ranch to the South Rim is a serious, long (9.7 miles) and strenuous hike… with an elevation increase of more than 4,500 feet." It went on to note, *"This hike should only be undertaken by those in very good physical condition."* The only thing they left out was an exclamation point. I got the feeling when reading that sentence—with its bold, underlined italics—that the author somehow saw my name on the passenger list and added the emphasis just for me.

O.A.R.S. has been hosting river trips through the Grand Canyon for decades. Over the years they've worked out every last detail to ensure the trip goes as smoothly as possible. One of those details is getting the duffel bags with our clothes and gear to the top of the canyon at the end of the trip. They arrange in advance for mules to take them. On the hike out of the canyon, we only had to carry a daypack with whatever we needed for the hike and for the time immediately following while we waited for the mules to reach the barn on the South Rim. That was a relief to learn. When we signed up for the trip, I thought we would have to carry all of our clothes and gear out of the canyon on our backs.

Most afternoons when we're not traveling, Karen and I walk for about an hour. We don't have a set time of day for our walks, but I've noticed that if I open the door to the kitchen pantry and reach for the potato chips, Karen immediately appears with her hiking shoes on, ready to walk out the door. I suspect she has a competition with herself to see how long she can make a bag of potato chips last in our house by distracting me with walks. I wonder what she would do if I took the bag of chips with us on our next walk. Anyway, our route is the same loop every day. At the far end, we pass a short trail known as Heart Attack Hill. It is aptly named.

Having committed to the river trip, it occurred to us that

maybe we should add Heart Attack Hill to our daily walk. It would only be another half of a mile, and the climb would be valuable training. It would also give us a sense of how we might fare on the hike out of the Grand Canyon. To our benefit, we were forced to hike down the hill first, and then back up to get home. Had it been the other way around, it would have been too easy for us to bail out after only climbing part way up the hill. Three weeks after we agreed to add Heart Attack Hill to our daily walk, and after walking past it twenty more times without doing it, we gave it a try.

"On these steep hills, I think the going down part is harder than the going up part," Karen said to me when we were halfway down the first time.

"I disagree. Going up seems much harder to me," I replied.

"I'm serious. It hurts my knees. Haven't I always said when we hike steep trails that it's harder to go down than up?"

"Yes, because you say that on the way down. You don't say anything on the way up because you're breathing too hard to speak."

There is a metal gate at the bottom of the hill. Without saying it to each other, we both understood that for the hike down and back to "count" you had to touch the gate before heading back up the hill. We both tapped the gate and began the climb. It was instantly much harder. I waited for just the right moment before continuing our discussion. That moment when Karen started breathing heavily, pressing her hands into her thighs, and leaning her shoulder into each step. "You're right, this is so much easier than coming down," I said.

"I have," she said while panting heavily.

"You what?"

"I have – three words for you."

[Loud wheeze.]

"Bite."

[Loud wheeze.]

"Me."

I'm still waiting for the third word.

We learned what we needed on that first try of Heart Attack Hill. It was time to get back into strenuous hiking shape. I wanted a comparison between Heart Attack Hill and the Phantom Ranch to South Rim hike, so I researched the length and elevation gain of Heart Attack Hill. That night at dinner I told Karen, "The good news, Sweetie, is that the hill we climbed today is twice as steep as the Grand Canyon hike. The bad news is it's about one-thirtieth the distance."

"How many times would we have to hike that hill to be the elevation gain equivalent of our Grand Canyon hike?"

"Heart Attack Hill is 300 feet elevation gain, so we'd have to do it fifteen times to equal the Grand Canyon hike."

"I'm taking a mule," she replied.

"I don't think that's an option."

"The mules are taking our duffel bags, why can't *I* take one up the canyon?"

"First, you are not a duffel bag, and second they don't have extra mules waiting around just in case someone doesn't want to do the hike."

"I can't reserve a mule?"

"No, you can't reserve a mule. It's not Avis."

"I think you're wrong. People ride the mules in the canyon all the time. I bet I could reserve a mule."

"You're not reserving a mule. Besides the fact that you can't, everyone would make fun of you. Don't you want to hike with the group?"

"I think I could talk the others into getting mules."

"OK, we're shutting down the mule talk. No one is riding mules out of the canyon."

It turns out Karen was right, and I was wrong. You can reserve a mule. I found this tidbit of information in a second document O.A.R.S. sent to us. It read, "While most people hike up to the South Rim, some people prefer riding passenger mules. Keep in mind that as a rider you must be in good physical condition. Riding requires upper and lower body strength as well as good overall muscular condition. The mule service costs approximately $850 (in 2016) for up to five riders, and you must reserve them in advance. If you decide on this option, you should make a reservation as soon as possible since they often book twelve months in advance." $850? For that, I'd carry Karen up the trail on my back.

I'm fairly sure Karen was joking about taking a mule. There were times though, in the months leading up to the trip, when she sounded serious. Thankfully—spoiler alert— no one, including Karen, rode a mule out of the canyon.

HAVASU FALLS

Heart Attack Hill was a wake-up call, and afterward, we began taking our conditioning more seriously. We planned training hikes with some of the other couples who were going on the river trip with us. On separate occasions, once with Craig and Aya and another time with our friends John and Lolly, we hiked Church Mountain in northern Washington State. With an elevation gain of 4,000 feet, it was a fair assessment of our physical readiness. Doing a hike like that and not being wiped out afterward gave us confidence that maybe we could manage the hike out of the Grand Canyon.

Karen got the idea that we should also do a practice hike in the Grand Canyon, but not in the national park. She wanted to hike to Havasu Falls on the Havasupai Indian Reservation just west of Grand Canyon National Park.

The location of the reservation can be confusing. Havasu Canyon is a side canyon leading to the Grand Canyon, but it isn't in Grand Canyon National Park. It also is not associated with—or anywhere near—Lake Havasu; the only thing these two places have in common is they are both in the state of Arizona. Lake Havasu is a reservoir about 170 miles southwest of the reservation.

The Havasupai Indians used to live on and farm land that's now within the boundaries of Grand Canyon National

Park. After the U.S. government formed the park, they restricted the Havasupai to a 518-acre reservation in Havasu Canyon. In 1975, Congress gave them back an additional 185,000 acres of canyon and rim territory. According to Stephen Hirst, author of *I Am the Grand Canyon: The Story of the Havasupai People*, the 2006 Havasupai census listed 684 persons of half or greater Havasupai ancestry. At that time, 454 of them resided on the Havasupai Indian Reservation.

The word "Havasupai" means people of the blue-green water. Havasu Falls and several other magnificent, turquoise blue waterfalls lie within the reservation. This is a place Karen has wanted to see for a long time; calling it a practice hike was just an excuse to go.

A couple of years before we booked the river trip, Karen and I made plans to hike to Havasu Falls in August, which we later found out is monsoon season. We'd booked a two-night stay in the small lodge in Supai Village, eight miles down from the trailhead. A few days before our scheduled hike, a flash flood devastated the village. Helicopters airlifted all of the residents to Red Cross shelters because the flood damaged their water and sewage systems. The lodge had no way to notify anyone that they were closed so we traveled all the way to the rim of the canyon before we learned what happened. Karen was very disappointed. She had written the Havasu Falls hike on an imaginary piece of paper and placed it in her imaginary wish bucket.

In the spring before our river trip, March 2016, we convinced John and Lolly to join us for another try. We were both lucky to get reservations at the lodge for the same night. The lodge sells outs months in advance, but we were able to get rooms due to late-date cancellations.

By coincidence, both Karen and I and John and Lolly had separately arranged to visit friends in Palm Springs over the weekend before our Havasu hike. I rented a car there, and we planned to pick up John and Lolly Monday morning and drive to Kingman, Arizona where we would spend the night at a Hampton Inn. On Tuesday morning we would drive from Kingman to the trailhead on the Havasupai Reservation and hike eight miles down to the village. We were eager to spend the rest of that day visiting the many falls further north of the village, stay the night at the lodge, and hike back to our car the next morning. Then, we would drive to Las Vegas and fly home from there.

The morning we left Palm Springs was delightful: sunny and mild, a perfect day for a drive. While eating breakfast on the back patio at our friend's house, Karen received a text from Lolly, "John's at the Urgent Care Clinic!" We've known John and Lolly for years, and we were certain she was joking—she wasn't.

"Hahahah," Karen texted back.

"Seriously. He's been there for a couple of hours," was Lolly's reply.

"What's wrong with him?"

"Not sure. His foot is swollen, and he's in a lot of pain."

Karen looked at me; she was devastated. "I can't believe it. Well, there goes Havasu Falls, again. This hike is jinxed."

A few minutes later Lolly texted again, "We should be ready to go in about an hour."

"What?! What about John's foot?" Karen replied.

"They prescribed pain medication. He's at the pharmacy. See you soon!"

We packed the car and headed out. I was sure we wouldn't be going to Kingman. Either that or the swollen foot thing was just a goof and John was fine.

When we got to the house where they were staying, we found John sitting on the back porch with his shoeless, swollen foot resting on the seat of a chair. His foot looked like he was wearing a tennis shoe with a sock over it; it was that swollen.

I said to John, "I'm sorry. Are we at the right place? This looks like a nursing home. John, can I get you some applesauce to take with your medication?"

John slowly stood up. His face grimaced. He hobbled one step toward us and said, "OK, let's go."

"Hold on sport. You don't look like you're in any shape to hike the Grand Canyon," I said.

Karen asked, "What happened to your foot?!"

"I don't know. It started hurting in the middle of the night, and by this morning I was in so much pain I went in to have it looked at. The doctor wasn't certain what it was, maybe a spider bite or a scorpion sting. Who knows?"

"You realize in twenty-four hours we're supposed to be starting an eight-mile hike into the desert, right? There's no way you'll make it," Karen said.

"They gave me pain pills. I'll be fine. Let's go."

John could barely walk to the car. Karen, Lolly and I exchanged confused looks. We had two options: drive to Las Vegas, prop John in front of a slot machine with pain pills and a two-gallon slushy-drink—the kind they put in a fake plastic guitar with a shoulder strap—and hang out there for a couple of days until our flight home, or drive to Kingman and reassess John's condition when we got there. We chose the second option. (I was kind of hoping the womenfolk had chosen Las Vegas. I've always wanted one of those guitar drinks.)

Our rental car had barely enough room for the four of us, our luggage and our backpacks. On top of that, John sat in the front passenger seat and put it in the fully reclined position. He was practically in Lolly's lap, who was in the seat behind him.

"John! Why do you need to put your seat so far back?" Lolly asked.

"I'm supposed to keep my foot elevated."

"Well, leaning back like that isn't elevating your foot. I can't breathe back here," she replied.

John didn't respond. Every ten minutes or so she would say, "John! How's the foot?" She never got more than an occasional, "Fine," out of him. It could have been the effect of the pain medication or maybe he was using his mystery illness as an excuse for not answering her. Either way, he faded in and out the entire way to Kingman, while Lolly and

Karen made plans for doing the hike regardless of whether John was well enough to go.

When we pulled into the Hampton Inn parking lot, Lolly said, "Oh look, there's a hospital right next door. We can leave you there tomorrow, John, if your foot isn't better." Karen nodded in agreement.

"Are you planning to wheel him over to the hospital and tell them we'll be back to pick him up in a couple of days?" I asked.

"Karen and I aren't going to miss the hike because of John's foot. We're going no matter what," Lolly replied.

"Nope. If John can't go, none of us are going." I was a little shocked I had to say that. John just sat there calmly listening to us argue and then said, "I'll be fine. I'm going on that hike tomorrow."

I had my doubts. John's foot looked bad, and the swelling wasn't going down.

Once we checked into the hotel, Karen and Lolly decided that we should go to Oyster's Mexican and Seafood for dinner. "We're going to a Mexican restaurant named Oyster's? Are oysters their specialty?" I asked. "The nearest ocean has to be 300 miles from here. I hope we don't regret this tomorrow in the middle of our hike."

The drive to the restaurant was short and even though we arrived at early bird hour (5:00 pm) the place was packed. We had an enjoyable dinner, most of which was spent listening to Lolly and Karen explain to John how much fun he'll have spending a couple of days at the hospital while we explore Havasu Falls. There was talk about sponge baths and extra pain medication if he behaved well. I held the line by repeating often, "If John can't go, none of us are going." Fortunately, my concerns about Oyster's were unfounded, the food and service were fantastic. And we had no regrets the next day.

When we got to the breakfast room the next morning, the first thing I saw was John drinking coffee; his foot was elevated on a chair. He had a shoe on his bum foot, but he hadn't laced it.

John said to Karen and me, "You guys look like your dog just died."

"We don't have a dog. How's the foot?" I asked.

"Still hurts, but it'll be fine."

"We're going for an long, difficult hike in three hours, and you can't tie your shoe. How is that going to be fine?"

"I'll manage."

It seemed ill-advised to me to hike into one of the most remote communities in the U.S. with an unknown injury. If we attempted the hike, but later, while in the middle of the Havasupai Reservation, John's mystery ailment flared up, we'd all be in trouble. We might need to life-flight him out of the canyon. That is, if we could get a signal to call Kingman. I was imagining being halfway down the trail—at the furthest point from any civilization or form of communication—and looking back to see John trailing far behind, dragging his bad leg behind him like a dead log, and saying "I'm fine. You guys keep going. I'll meet you at the village." There might even be a stray dog nipping at it, but he wouldn't notice because he had lost all feeling in that leg. That's when I'd have to put his sorry ass on my back and carry him out of the canyon. The whole time I would have to listen to him say, "I'm fine. Put me down."

Since he was still insisting we go on with the hike, I suggested to the group that we pack, check out of the hotel and drive to the trailhead. We could always turn back later if needed.

From Kingman, we drove east on Arizona Highway 66 (part of the original Route 66) toward Peach Springs. About fifty miles outside of Kingman we turned north on Indian Road 18 and followed it sixty desolate miles until it ended at the trailhead. We were surprised to see at least a couple of hundred cars in the parking lot. Despite the large number, we were able to find a place to shoehorn our car in along the shoulder of the road.

We all piled out and began unloading our packs from the

trunk. John groaned as he got out of the car, but didn't say a word. By that point, we all concluded if he couldn't do the hike, he'd let us know. There was no sense asking him over and over. Karen and Lolly quickly started an assembly line to make sandwiches, and I dug through my pack to get a complete accounting of how much water I had. There's no potable water on the trail, and we didn't have a water filter with us. Everyone double-checked their packs, grabbed their trekking poles and waited while I put the stuff we were leaving behind into the trunk and locked the car. We started walking toward the trailhead; John brought up the rear limping.

The trail descended immediately. We weren't thirty yards into the hike when I noticed John had stopped, so we all stopped. I thought, "Uh-oh, here we go. Time to head back to the car."

"John!" barked Lolly.

"Hold on, hold on," he replied.

"John! Come on!"

"Hold on!"

Lolly continued to bark at John, and John continued ignoring her for a couple of minutes. "Do you need us to get you a wheelchair, John," I hollered.

"All three of you need to just calm down. You guys need the pain medication more than I do. I'm resetting my GPS and have to wait for it to find the satellites."

The first mile and a half of the trail were essentially stairs. I was at the front of the group, and every time I looked back to check on John, I was surprised at how close he was. It was as if his foot was perfectly fine. Had I not seen his swollen foot with my own eyes, I would swear he had been playing a practical joke on us. When we got to the bottom of the mile and a half steep section of the trail I heard John shout, "Wait! Wait a minute!"

"What's wrong, John?" I asked.

He was looking at his GPS. "It says we've already come down 1,000 feet in elevation and we still have another six and a half miles to the village."

"Yeah."

"Karen told Lolly that this entire hike was only 750-foot elevation change. That's the only reason I agreed to this."

Karen said, "I meant this first part was only 750 feet."

"Well, you lied about that because we've already come down 1,000 feet. What's the elevation change from here to the village?" John asked Karen.

"About another 1,000 feet."

"Another 1,000 feet!"

John's good-natured complaining was an encouraging sign; his foot must have been feeling better. For the rest of the trip, an hour didn't pass without hearing, "The Smiths are liars," from John. Most of the time he added expletives.

"Not the Smiths, just Karen," I kept reminding him.

The first mile and a half was steep, but the remaining six and a half miles were a gradual downhill grade. Mostly, we were alone on the trail. Even though it was the beginning of spring break and the parking lot was crowded, we didn't see many other hikers. We fell into a peaceful rhythm while hiking through the wash, making slow, steady progress. No one spoke. John was still limping slightly, but keeping up with the group.

About halfway to the village, I thought I heard a person in the distance shouting. I couldn't tell if the sound was coming from in front of us or behind us. A minute later I heard it again, followed by a loud whistle. Then the ground began to rumble. At the time, we were hiking along the inside curve of a bend in the canyon. We couldn't see around the corner, but by then it was apparent that the noise was coming from in front of us. The rumble quickly got stronger, dust started flying, and there was another loud shout and whistle. I'd never heard or felt anything like that on a trail before. In an instant, a dozen or so horses raced past us; a single horseman was bringing up the rear. It was like a scene out of a cowboy movie. We jumped out of the way just in time, lucky that the horses didn't trample us.

When the dust settled we looked at each other with open mouths. "What the hell was that?" I said. "I think those horses would have run right through us if we hadn't moved."

"I think you're right," John replied. "We need to pay attention. There's probably more coming." There were.

Since there are no roads to Supai Village, there are only three ways to get food and supplies down there: helicopter, on the back of a mule or horse, or carry it yourself. The mule and horse trains are constantly carrying stuff between the trailhead and the village. It's the only place in the U.S. that receives mail by mule. Every letter and package sent from Supai Village has a special postmark with mules on it.

The last mile or so of the hike was in shade. The grade flattened, and we walked beneath tall, leafy trees next to the blue water of Havasu Creek. We arrived at the village and walked down the main dirt road until we found the lodge, which was a two-story motel with 24 rooms. A sign on the office door said check-in time was at 1:00 pm, so we went to the visitor center to get our permit. Once we showed the ranger our reservations for the lodge, he gave us an orange tag that indicated we had a permit to visit the falls. We were required to have the permit on us and visible while in the village and on the trails to the falls. In fact, the Havasupai only allow visitors to the area who have a reservation for the campgrounds or the lodge; they do not allow day hikes.

While we were in the visitor center we saw a ranger talking with a couple—a man and a woman—who had hiked down from the trailhead. Apparently they were just learning about the "no day hike" rule. It looked like an awkward conversation. We couldn't hear everything being said, but the ranger was essentially telling them, "Sorry, that's the rule. No reservation, no permit."

The man asked, "So, we hiked all of the way down here and now we have to turn right around and hike back without seeing the falls?"

I could see the expression on the woman's face. At first she was glaring at the ranger, shocked at what he was telling her, but soon she turned her gaze toward her partner. "Uh-oh, he's in trouble," I thought. I recognized the look on her face. It was the "how could you be so stupid" look. I've been on the receiving end of that a few times.

We were anxious to see the falls, but it was close to 1:00, so we hung around the lobby of the lodge. Lolly and I formed a line at the front desk about fifteen minutes before the workers showed up to check in guests. The entire time we were waiting, we could hear the front desk phone ringing. The sound of the endless rings reminded me of the many times I had called to make a reservation and no one picked up.

When it came time, Lolly checked in first and used her credit card to pay. The front desk clerk took her card and swiped it on a machine mounted to the back wall of the office. It was an old dial-up system, and it took several minutes for the call to go through and for the verification to print. I was ready to check in next, but before the clerk took my credit card she answered the front desk phone. When she ended the conversation, instead of putting the phone back on the receiver, she placed it on the desk and started checking me in. I could hear a busy signal now coming from the handset sitting on the desk. When the clerk tried to run my credit card it failed to make a connection. She looked at me and said, "This machine is down right now. Our phone line must be down. I'll have to try your card again in a few minutes."

I thought to myself, "Or, maybe your one line is busy because you haven't hung up the phone yet." I didn't want to tell them how to run their business, so even though it took all of my self-control, I politely waited. For about ten minutes I watched while the clerks tried to check in the other guests. Each time the credit card machine failed to connect. All the while there was the faint sound of a busy signal in the air.

Finally, one of the workers hung up the phone. Miraculously, the credit card machine started working. I said to Lolly as we walked out, "This entire lodge is running off of that one phone line. No wonder it's so difficult to get in touch with them from the outside."

When we got to our rooms, we emptied our packs of everything we wouldn't need on our hike to the falls. The rooms were spartan, but they had the essentials: two beds, a flush toilet, and a window unit air conditioner.

Havasu Falls may be the main attraction, but there are several other falls along Havasu Creek that are spectacular. From the village, we walked north on Havasu Creek Trail. We first came to a series of falls that required a short side-trip to see: Fiftyfoot Falls, Rock Falls, and Navajo Falls. We stopped to take photos, but when John, Lolly, and Karen started hiking again, I didn't follow them. I was about a hundred yards from the creek and could see two people standing in the water at the top of Fifty-Foot Falls. While there are signs strictly prohibiting visitors from jumping off the falls and cliffs into the water, people still do it, often.

I couldn't look away. I got out my phone and began taking a video of the couple at the top of the falls. A minute passed, and just as I started to have doubts that they would have the nerve to jump, the woman leaped. I heard cheering and clapping downstream. When I pointed my phone in the directions of the cheering, I saw several swimmers sitting on rocks by the side of the creek. They had been encouraging her to jump.

We continued to hike for another mile or so to the top of Havasu Falls. There is a spot to view the falls from above, although the "money-shot"—as Karen calls it—is from below. The trail takes you down to the bottom, and from there you can walk around the pool below the falls.

When you see photos of the falls you might think, like I did, that the color of the water in the photos has been enhanced, because it couldn't possibly be that blue. It is. A unique combination of minerals and lighting conditions cause the water to appear turquoise. It's an incredible sight.

Mooney Falls is further north along the trail. On our way there, we walked through the campgrounds, which were packed with young people on spring break. Some of them gave us curious looks as we walked past; they were probably wondering, "Dude! Who brought their parents?" We were easily twice as old as most of the campers, and wearing twice as many clothes. On average, the Havasupai issue permits for 300 campers per day, but we've read that the numbers can swell to 500 during holidays and spring break.

Mooney is every bit as spectacular as Havasu Falls. The only catch is that the hike to the bottom of the falls is very steep and requires that you hold onto chains, ladders, and bolts while descending a 200-foot cliff. It made me extremely nervous, not just the steepness of the hike or the heights, but the crowds of people who were simultaneously trying to go down while others were trying to come up. It looked like an accident waiting to happen.

As a matter of fact, the falls are named after a prospector—Daniel Mooney—who fell to his death in the late 1800s while trying to get to the base of the falls. The story goes, he couldn't find a trail to the bottom, so he attempted to rappel down. As he was descending, the sharp rocks on the side of the cliff severed his rope and he fell to his death. Afterward, his fellow miners learned of a path used by the locals to get to the bottom. That trail proved to be too treacherous for their liking, so they blasted a couple of tunnels to make it safer. Today, those same tunnels are part of the trail to the bottom, although the chains and iron handholds have also been added for safety.

We decided to turn back toward the village when we reached the top of Mooney Falls. However, *had* we braved the climb down to the bottom of Mooney, we could have continued north a couple more miles to Beaver Falls. And a few miles beyond that is the Colorado River. We'd read that it is possible to hike all the way to the Colorado River from Beaver Falls, but the trail is less established and could at times require creek crossings and a bit of bushwhacking.

As we started back up the trail, a young woman, who was in a hurry to get around us on her way toward Mooney Falls, stepped aside to let us pass. As I carefully slid past her, I could see her bare feet standing on the edge of a rock. The drop-off directly below where she was standing was at least fifty feet—that's like standing on the edge of a five-story building with no railing. Had I slipped and bumped her, had she slipped and fallen, had anything happened right at that moment to cause her to fall off her perch, she would have been a goner, and I would have spent the rest of the week being interviewed by the tribal police. They would interrogate Karen separately to determine if I may have pushed the woman off the cliff. They'd ask, "Has your husband ever exhibited signs of anti-social behavior?"

She would reply, "Um, could you please define anti-social?"

It was good we got out of there before someone got hurt.

Besides my concern about the crowds on the trail, we were tired. It had been a long day, we had several miles to hike back to the village, and we hadn't brought much in the way of food for dinner. Supai has a convenience store and a snack bar. Our hope was the snack bar would still be open by the time we made it back. The sign read, "Open 'til 6:00 pm" when we walked past it earlier in the day, but there was one small problem: we didn't know which time zone we were in. I'm never certain what time it is when I'm in Arizona, especially around the change from daylight savings time and standard time. Arizona, along with Indiana, doesn't change their clocks, they change their time zone. That's easy enough to remember, but do the Havasu follow Arizona's time zone? The Navajo don't. Between the delirium of having hiked too long and our ignorance about what time it was, we didn't know if we had an hour to get back to the village or two. Either way, John and I didn't want to miss out on fry bread, so we picked up our pace.

Karen and Lolly were not as enthusiastic about hiking quickly, uphill, for three miles after having already trudged fourteen miles. Karen kept assuring John and me, "We have plenty of time, relax."

How could she be so sure? "There's fry bread at stake. Fry bread!"

The last we saw of Karen and Lolly they were taking their hiking boots and socks off and putting their feet into the creek. Neither John or I broke stride or said a word to each other when they stopped. We knew what we had to do.

By the time we reached the snack bar, I was limping worse than John. We'd hiked seventeen miles and hit our limit. Surprisingly, we weren't there but a couple of minutes when Karen and Lolly arrived. I never learned for sure what time it was. It no longer mattered; the snack bar was open and taking orders. For such a remote place, they had a wide variety of choices: burgers, burritos, grilled cheese, chicken sandwiches, chili, and yes—fry bread.

Once the snack bar closed, there was nowhere else to go and nothing to do in the village. It would have been great to have a cold beer, but like many Indian reservations, Havasu is dry; they don't allow alcohol, anywhere. The lodge had no TV, Internet, or cell service, so we went to John and Lolly's room to play cards. That's when John sat down, took off his hiking boots, and rested his sore foot on a chair. We were stunned to see his foot was nearly as swollen as the day before.

"John, your foot is still huge!" Karen said.

"Yeah, it hurts pretty bad," he said.

"I can't believe you were able to hike seventeen miles like that."

"I had my doubts as well, but I didn't want to let you down. I knew this has been on your bucket list for a long time and I wasn't going to be the reason that it fell through a second time."

Karen was touched. "Let me get you a pillow for your foot," she said.

"Um, my feet hurt pretty bad also," I said, but that drew no reaction from the gals, not even a glance my way. I had to let John be the hero for the moment. I knew it would wear off soon.

The next morning, we got up early so we could finish the hike out before the warmest part of the day. Our room was adjacent to John and Lolly's, and we woke to the sound of Lolly shrieking. It wasn't a long shriek; it sounded more like a yelp or a whoop. "What's going on over there? I'm glad we got separate rooms," I thought. Later, we learned that she had been taking a cold shower. It wasn't her intention; there was no hot water. I figured that might have been the case after I ran the hot water in our room for a few minutes, and it never got warmer than the water coming out of the cold side of the faucet. That made it an easy decision to skip bathing for the day.

The weather was pleasant on our hike out. We were fortunate to have had two good days in a row. The gradual uphill grade for the first six and a half miles made it easy to forget that we'd come up 1,000 feet of elevation. Not so for the last mile and a half. There is a distinct beginning to the steep section of the trail, like starting up a flight of stairs. Reaching this spot brought back the complaints from John, "I'm never trusting Karen again," and so on. Mercifully, he was soon breathing too hard to bitch. We all plodded up the trail, each at different speeds and met at the top.

John paused for a long time looking at his GPS then announced that we'd hiked twenty-six miles in twenty-six hours. Not a bad practice for our Bright Angel hike. A day earlier I would never have guessed John would be able to walk that far with his swollen foot.

On our drive out we were already talking about doing the hike again in the future. Maybe next time we'd get more couples to join us. The only change I would make—other than John not getting bit by a spider or stung by a scorpion the day before the hike—is to spend two nights in the lodge or at the campgrounds. You need a full day to explore the falls on fresh legs. (John never learned the cause of the swelling in his foot.)

Havasu Canyon. View from half way down the initial steep section of the trail.

Havasu Falls
(to see color versions of our photos visit www.doriesho.com)

PARTY

Karen felt we needed to host a pre-trip get-together at our house with the couples joining us on the trip because not all of Craig and Aya's friends knew all of our friends.

"I'll buy the same box wine that we'll be drinking on the river so we can test it and decide what to order," Karen said.

"You have to test the wine?" I responded.

"Yeah! We can't just show up on the river and not know if the wine we ordered is any good. They offer six varieties to choose from: Chardonnay, Pinot Grigio, Sauvignon Blanc, Cabernet, Merlot, and Malbec. I'm buying a box of each for the party so we can have a wine tasting."

"Six boxes? Doesn't each box hold three liters? That's the same as four bottles. You'd be wine tasting your way through twenty-four bottles of wine!"

"And your point is?"

"I'm not sure we need to have everyone over to our house for that."

"Also, you guys need to decide what beer you'll be drinking on the river. O.A.R.S. only transports canned beer."

"Are you suggesting we have a party so the guys can practice drinking beer out of a can? Now *that* makes sense. You should have started with that as your reason for the party."

In O.A.R.S.' pre-trip literature, there was a notice that said, "National Park Service regulations prevent us from providing alcoholic beverages to our guests. You are welcome to bring a supply of alcoholic beverages in non-breakable containers or you can order them using the beer/wine order form which will be sent to you with your final invoice. *Please Note: There is no drinking allowed while on the river. Consumption of alcoholic beverages is only allowed while in camp.*"

A few months before the river trip, four of the couples came to our house for a party. The other three couples lived out of state and couldn't make it. We invited others as well. I had assumed our friends who weren't going on the trip with us knew about our upcoming Grand Canyon expedition. They didn't.

My toast to a safe Grand Canyon trip was barely out of my mouth when I heard one of our guests turn to Karen and say, "The *what* trip? What is he talking about?" Karen looked in my direction for help, but I weaseled my way across the room. There was no use in both of us getting caught in an embarrassing conversation. I was confident Karen could handle it.

Karen replied, "Uh, well, the float trip through the Grand Canyon?"

"You're floating the Colorado River? We've always wanted to do that! Is it just you and Matt?"

"Uh, no, uh, John and Lolly are also going."

"I thought I heard Craig say something like 'can't wait' after Matt's toast. Are they going?"

"Well, yeah, Craig and Aya are also going. Yep. And Steve and Cindy. And Phill and Wendy."

"Wow." Long, awkward pause, "Did you guys just plan this?"

"Uh, no, it's been planned for awhile. About a year and a half."

Karen didn't wait for more follow up questions. She launched into her explanation about there being only sixteen spaces available and everyone we'd initially invited said yes and how we wish more friends could come, yada, yada, yada. We had become well practiced at this speech.

If Karen senses the other person is still pissed off because we didn't ask them to go, she makes one last effort to make them feel better by downplaying the trip. "Don't feel bad, you probably wouldn't like it anyway. There'll be snakes down there; the boats might flip and you could drown; you wouldn't be able to wash your hair for a week; everyone has to poop in a bucket..." If I'm standing there, I usually pull Karen away by the arm when she gets to the 'poop in a bucket' part and say, "Let it go, Sweetie. They hate us now."

The hors d'oeuvre table at our campsite. O.A.R.S. removed the bags of wine from their boxes and placed them into canvas holders that hung by a strap. Each one was labeled with the initials of the person who ordered it.

ON THE ROAD AGAIN

In September 2016, we began our journey to Flagstaff where the river trip began. We left a week early and traveled with John and Lolly to several national parks along the way.

For Karen and I, every road trip is different, yet there's a pattern that they all follow, at least for the first day of travel. There are many stages to the start of a trip; the first is packing.

We pack as differently as two people could. I have my master list, and Karen has, well, I don't know what Karen has, but she seems to manage to get all of her stuff together by the time we pull away from the house. I've tried without success to convince her that she needs to make a list. As I am packing and come across items I know she needs to be reminded of, the conversation is always the same.

"Headlamp. Karen, did you remember to pack your headlamp? Because, you know, there are a lot of things we can share and a headlamp isn't one of them." I say this so she'll remember the conversation a week later when she turns to me and asks, "Where's *our* headlamp?"

Her response to my reminders is always the same: a dismissive, "I got it."

"You got it? What does, 'I got it' mean? Did you write it down? Where's your list?"

She puts her index finger to her head and says, "I got it right here." She never points to the same spot on her head when she says this.

"What does that mean? Is it in your hair? Is it on your forehead? The universal sign for 'it's in my memory' is this." I tap my temple as I'm saying this.

"You just worry about where your memory is, and I'll worry about mine," she says.

"OK, but, we—can't—share—a headlamp."

The next stage is getting the car ready, or in the case of our drive to the Grand Canyon, the truck. Depending on the length of the trip, this stage might involve having the oil changed or the next major service performed at the dealership. It certainly includes washing the vehicle, which usually hasn't been done since the previous trip, checking the tire pressure and filling it with gas. The truck must be filled with gas when we pull away from home. Having to stop for gas after two miles is a buzzkill.

Filling up the truck with gas for a road trip is not the same as an everyday fill-up. It requires that I go into the gas station's food mart and peruse the aisles just in case I've forgotten something. Ice, Water, Pringles, Nilla Wafers, Imodium AD, the essentials. Ohhhh, toasted coconut mini-donuts? Hmmm, there's probably no way to hide these in the truck and eat them later without Karen seeing me, I'll pass. At a minimum, I'll purchase a small bag of Cheez-Its (just in case something happens to the unopened box of Cheez-Its I already have in the truck) and a $2 scratch-off lottery ticket.

With the truck gassed up, I can move on to the loading stage. A few years ago when we put our old family car out to pasture, we bought our pickup truck. It's perfect for road trips, but it enables my OC behavior by allowing me to be even more overprepared than before. The amount of unnecessary stuff I bring with us on a trip has expanded to fill the larger capacity of our new vehicle.

The closer we get to our departure time the more frantic the dialogue in my head becomes. "Should I bring a hammer?

45

Sure, might need a hammer. How about a small shovel in case we get stuck in the snow? Sure, we need a small shovel." Of course, a small shovel would only be useful if we got stuck in just the right amount of snow that wouldn't require a full-sized shovel; a condition that will only present itself once in my lifetime, and most likely on the first trip when I don't bring my small shovel. "Washer fluid? Yep. Tire chains? Yep. Gloves to wear when putting on the tire chains? Of course!" It's endless.

I prefer to have containers for all my stuff: backpack, suitcase, ditty bags, etc. Everything has a place, and everything is in its place. Karen is very organized when it comes to packing her suitcase, but everything else is in a pile. The pile starts growing by the front door of our house several days before the trip: backpacks (a large one and a small one), hiking boots, tennis shoes, water sandals, trekking poles, raincoat, fleece jacket, fleece vest, down jacket, down vest... There is no telling how large it'll get. I shouldn't complain about how much stuff she brings on our driving trips when I've filled the bed of the truck with unnecessary garden tools. But her pile can get large.

Eventually, Karen has everything she intends to bring with her by the front door. There is one, and only one sign that indicates her pile is finished: she places her hair straightener on top. When I see the electrical cord dangling down the side of the mound, I know it's time to hit the road.

Years ago we adopted a family rule: you-pack-it-you-carry-it. This gives the packer an incentive to be thoughtful about what he or she brings on a trip. There are no hard feelings. Everyone (Karen) knows the rule. I'm not un-chivalrous (although I'm sure I will get emails to the contrary). It is a family rule and is one of the many reasons why we have such harmonious travels.

However, there is one time when the you-pack-it-you-carry-it rule does not apply. That's during the loading phase of the trip. I load. This hasn't always been the case. We've tried a you-pack-it-you-load-it rule, but that resulted in

Karen's stuff taking up three-fourths of the back seat. I've made an effort to explain to Karen that half of the back seat is hers and half is mine, but she gets stuck on the word "half." Half to her is not so much a math concept as it is "the amount of space I need to pile my shit into the backseat."

I do the loading to defend my territory more than anything. Snacks and water go in the middle forming a friendly demarcation of the respective *halves* of the backseat. From there, Karen's stuff has to fit on her half, and my stuff has to fit on my half. Since I am the sole loader, I can also hide some of my stuff under Karen's. It usually takes a couple of days for her to ask, "Why is there a small shovel under my backpack?" Also, I can make sure that the electrical cord to her hair straightener makes it all the way into the truck. I don't want the end of the cord flapping in the wind and dinging the side of the truck—again.

On this trip, I was almost finished loading the truck when Karen came onto the driveway and said, "Stop! Stop! I want to take a picture of our stuff before you load the truck."

"You want to what?"

"We're going on an epic trip, and I want to take a picture. It'll be great. I'll put the snacks in front so everyone can see your animal crackers and Cheez-Its."

Karen has an Instagram addiction. Not only would it be a tremendous waste of time and energy to unload the truck and then immediately reload it, I felt that by refusing, I was helping her tame her compulsion.

"I'm not unloading the truck *now*, that would be…" I caught myself before I said "stupid."

"That would be what?" Karen asked, with a slight turn of her head.

"Sweetie, we are five minutes from driving away. Road trip! Yay! Let's go!" I was trying to distract her. She wouldn't be. She sulked for a couple of minutes then snapped back to her usual, cheerful self.

I loaded the piles and threw an extra hammer in the back of the truck. It was time for stage four: leaving the house. For everyone else, leaving the house might not be considered a stage, but for us, it always seems to take longer than it should.

"Which lights should we leave on while we're gone?" Karen asks.

"I don't care, you decide." It's been my reply for every trip we've ever taken.

"Should we leave a light on in the bedroom?" she asks. This is what she does. When I say I don't care, she asks the same question in different ways until I do care, which I never do.

"Sweetie, I don't care if we leave a light on in the bedroom," I respond.

"Should we leave the outside lights on?" Before I can say, "I don't care," she says, "But then they'll be on during the day, and it'll look like we're not home."

"I don't care."

"If we don't leave lights on someone will rob us."

"I'm not as convinced of that as you…"

"Should we leave a light on in the kitchen?"

This is usually the point when I realize there is only one way for this to end, "Yes, definitely, we should leave a light on in the kitchen. That's a good idea, a really good idea. I'm glad you thought of that. I wouldn't have thought of that. Good catch, Sweetie." I have to be careful though. If I'm too enthusiastic, she knows I'm just saying whatever I think will get us on the road as quickly as possible.

We double check every lock on every door, turn a few more lights on, turn a couple of them back off, close one blind, open another, put the last dirty glass in the dishwasher, reprogram the thermostat, unplug the coffeemaker and any other device Karen walks past on her way to the door, and then we're ready. And how do I know we are truly ready? I get an enthusiastic, "It's time to get this party started," from my lovely wife.

Driving away. Driving away is the fifth stage. Sometimes it takes a few tries before it sticks. Our first stop is at the end of the driveway so Karen can look back to see if we've left a window open and to make sure the house isn't on fire. If all is well, we can pull out into the road, which is when the load begins to shift. As long as I don't hear glass breaking or liquid running, I consider the load shifting a success.

But we haven't officially left yet. We must go back home a few minutes later to retrieve the thing we forgot. Sometimes the thing is truly important like my wallet, or my laptop, or my national parks passport. Sometimes we go back home because my OC flares up.

"I think we should bring a hammer with us. It'll just take a second to go back and get one," I say to Karen.

She doesn't respond. She has concluded that letting me feed the OC beast is the fastest way to get back on the road.

The next stage doesn't have a name, but it's a stage we cannot skip, or it's not an official road trip. Karen waits until we get at least a couple of miles away from our house, a safe enough distance that she's confident we aren't going back for another hammer. And then she sings the Willie Nelson song, *On the Road Again.* "On the road again" are the only words she sings. (I'm sure they're the only ones she knows.) She follows these four words with a series of guitar twang sounds, "Neer neer neer na-neer..." We've never discussed this, but I know she expects me to join along with her at the "neer neer neer na-neer" part of the song, which I never do. It's not because I don't want to. It's because she times her singing to the precise moment when I need to cross seven lanes of rush hour traffic in the next 300 yards to make it to our off-ramp, so we don't have to take a thirty-minute detour to get out of town.

I'm now labeled a spoilsport and Karen is quiet until we die in a car crash or I make it across all seven lanes of traffic and give her a heartfelt, "Neer neer neer na-neer." One time I responded to her by singing, "Like a band a gypsies we go down the highway," and she gave me a look that said, "What's that? You're supposed to sing 'neer neer neer na-neer.'" I won't make that mistake again. Now, I keep to the script so we can get to the next stage: snack time.

There have been trips when we've eaten all of our salty snacks for the entire trip in the first hour. Hence, the emergency bag of Cheez-Its. The only reason it didn't happen on this trip is because we had a *lot* of snacks. We were driving to the Grand Canyon and back, the Grand Canyon! In such a situation I'm compelled to open every bag and box of snacks early in the trip and sample each, so I know my options.

Most of the time, Karen only eats healthy foods. But on a road trip, her defenses are weak. More often than not, when I reach into the bag of chips while driving, the first thing I feel is her hand. Even though I've explained this a hundred times, Karen doesn't seem to grasp the concept that I cannot look at the bag of chips and keep my eye on the road at the same time. So, when she moves the bag, and then I place my hand where the bag was a minute ago she always asks, "What are you looking for?"

"The chips," I say.

"They're right here," she says with a hint of irritation.

"Sweetie, I don't know where 'right here' is. I have to keep my eyes on the road." This never draws a response. Sometimes I hear the bag rustle, and I can only assume she is placing it back in the general vicinity of where it was before this silly conversation started.

Aside from the fact that I can't drive and search for the snacks at the same time, sometimes I *can* see with my peripheral vision that she's dropped something (a snack item) between her seat and the center console of the truck.

"Are you going to get that?" I ask.

"I thought you couldn't see over here."

"I could see out of the corner of my eye the chip falling and you glancing into the crack."

"It's gone."

"What do you mean it's gone? You didn't even try to get it."

I hear heavy sighs and what sounds like a mild attempt at retrieving the lost snack, and then she says, "Nope. It's gone."

"OK, it didn't disappear. It's down there somewhere." I have to admit it's difficult to reach something if it falls into the crack of my truck.

Karen looks one more time then says with relief, "I see it. It's in the back seat."

"Are you going to get it?" I ask.

With shrugged shoulders and raised highbrows she repeats, "It's in the back seat." She says this as if it's now out of her jurisdiction, as in, "I'd like to get it, but it's in the back seat. Nothing I can do about it."

And so snack time goes until we are so thirsty that we can't stand it anymore. We put away the snacks, and Karen digs out a couple of bottles of water from the back seat. That's right. With one arm and without looking she can feel her way through the four layers of bags, blankets, pillows, luggage, and hammers stacked in the back to retrieve a bottle of water, but she can't get the chip.

The next stage is car dancing, followed by naptime, not for me, but for Karen. She puts on her sunglasses, takes a nap and denies it. When she wakes up, she's either too hot or too cold. On this trip, she immediately tried to change the radio station when she woke up from her nap. After her third attempt, I asked, "What are you doing?" I knew what she was doing; I wanted to hear her say it.

"I'm cold. I'm turning up the heat," she says.

I paused and did my best to keep my composure, and then said, "You know that's the radio knob, right?" These are the moments a husband lives for.

The final stage is the "settle in" stage when we mostly just want to reach our destination as soon as possible. On the first day of our road trip to the Grand Canyon, we drove from Seattle to Missoula, Montana. The drive took about eight hours. John and Lolly drove separately, and we were never more than ten miles behind them the entire way. We arrived at the Hampton Inn in Missoula early enough to have dinner together.

Like many small towns that are home to a university,

Missoula is a vibrant town and seems to be ahead of the times. College town aside, I'm basing this judgment mostly on the number and quality of their breweries.

We found an excellent restaurant in the downtown area and had a enjoyable dinner, just the four of us. We were buzzing with excitement about the river trip, the kind of excitement you feel at the start of a long-anticipated, extraordinary journey.

There was one piece of business we had to finish before going back to the Hampton Inn. All of the couples had agreed that we would bring gifts for the boatmen and crew that we would present to them on our last night on the river. These gifts weren't replacing a cash tip; they were meant to be a personal gesture of thanks.

Neither Karen and I nor John and Lolly had gotten a gift yet, so we walked to Stockman's Bar after dinner to see if they sold any interesting souvenirs that would suffice. Stockman's has been owned and operated by the same family for over sixty years. It's an institution in Missoula and famous for their slogan, "Liquor up front, poker in the rear." John and I were juvenile enough to insist we get our gifts at Stockman's emblazoned with their catchy phrase. John bought a t-shirt, and I bought a belt buckle that doubled as a whiskey flask. We were very proud of our purchases, Karen and Lolly not so much.

MORNINGS ON THE ROAD

I woke the next morning to the light of an iPad shining in my face. Usually, I'm the one who wakes up first each morning. On those rare occasions when Karen beats me to it, she uses a progression of techniques to wake me.

First, she tries to roust me by reading her iPad in bed. She knows I'm sensitive to light when I sleep. The light from her device is usually enough to wake me as it did that morning.

Most nights, after we turn out the lights in our hotel room, I have to get up and cover all of the LEDs on the electronics: smoke detectors, clock radios, and microwaves. TVs are the worst; they usually have a red light *and* a green light that shine like laser beams keeping me awake. If I don't cover them, I spend the night dreaming that a plane is coming in for a landing in our room.

There was a time when my obsession with lights at night drove Karen nuts. She thought I was being difficult for the sake of being difficult. I believe the word she used was fastidious, whatever that means. She would say, "Why don't you try sleeping with your eyes closed?" My sensitivity to light was a constant source of ridicule until one night I awoke to a loud, "Damn it!"

I searched in the bed next to me and only found an empty, warm spot where Karen had been sleeping. I heard her knock her water bottle off the table across the room, and then loudly exhale in frustration.

"What's wrong?" I asked.

"I stubbed my foot on the dresser."

"Why are you walking around in the dark?"

"I'm trying to cover the lights on the TV. They're keeping me awake. Where's that small role of duct tape you always bring with you?"

"Why don't you try sleeping with your eyes closed?" I knew if I lived long enough I would get to use that line on her. I wasn't about to search for my duct tape in the middle of the night. I don't know what happened next because I was asleep, but since then I'm no longer ridiculed for my room-darkening activities each night. Rather, she uses my light irritation to her advantage, like reading her iPad in bed to wake me. I caught her once pointing both her phone *and* iPad at me when she thought I was sound asleep.

If a few minutes of light shining doesn't get me up she moves on to yawning and jostling the bed. The yawns get progressively louder and protracted until she sounds like a moose in distress. Nearly always I'm awake by this point, but I don't move or open my eyes because the performance is too entertaining to interrupt.

Next, a hand comes over to my side of the bed patting the covers as if she's checking to see if anyone is there. Her searching progresses to a level of forcefulness that would rouse anyone unless they were dead. I sometimes stay still during this phase in an attempt to make her think I'm truly dead, which she never does.

Finally, in a loud voice, she announces, "I guess I'll have to get the coffee today." She never gets the coffee. No matter how long I continue to act like I'm sleeping, she waits me out. Then I get coffee.

Coffee in bed is one of our favorite times of the day. It's calm and peaceful. We check email and take care of any business we can electronically. It's when we talk about the plan for the day. Coffee time is so peaceful I'm often tempted to take my first nap of the day then. I do this however at the risk of being awoken by the sound of Karen taking a shower.

Each morning in our hotel room there is a competition between Karen and me for who takes a shower first. It's not a race; it's more like a chess match. Sure, I could jump out of bed and beat her to the shower, but I would be short-changing my coffee time. To most, being the first to shower in the morning might not seem like something worth worrying about. Most don't travel with Karen.

When Karen showers first, she has a head start at getting dressed. When Karen is fully dressed, she's ready to embrace the day. And embracing the day begins with opening the curtains to our hotel room. She throws them aside, spins around dramatically, holds one arm out as if she's a game show hostess displaying a new car and says, "Look! It's a beautiful day!"

For years I would say to her, "Please do *not* open the curtains while I'm in the shower. I don't want to come out of the bathroom and have the world see me naked." And even though I've always asked nicely, I would come out with a towel around my waist and wave to the family of four loading their minivan right outside our room. Why would I do this? Because the curtains would be open!

"Why don't you get dressed in the bathroom?" she would ask.

"Why don't you wait until I have clothes on before opening the curtains?"

"Because it's a beautiful day!"

"I don't want to get dressed in there. It's all steamy and hot. There's no dry place to put my clean clothes while I'm showering. I'd rather get dressed out here."

We've repeated our curtain argument for years. Then there was the period when Karen would open the room-darkening curtains but leave the sheer curtains closed. She thought this was a reasonable compromise. I assured her that this still counted as opening the curtains, which she denied. I proved her wrong by waving to the family of four loading their minivan right outside our window, and they sheepishly waved back.

Finally, I had to do it, the nuclear option. I didn't want to, but she forced my hand. I waited until we were staying in a ground floor room and getting a late start, so there was a chance of activity outside our window, and then I opened the curtains while she was in the shower.

"Close the curtains! I'm not dressed!"

"Look," I said. "It's a beautiful day!" I even did the game show hostess thing with my arm.

"I'm not dressed, close them!"

I left the curtains open and said, "Just get dressed in the bathroom. Hey, I'm going to the lobby to get more coffee. Do you want any?"

It was worth it just to watch her slide along the wall of the room trying to get to the curtains and close them before anyone saw her. We then called a truce. Now, we have an understanding. We both have to agree when it's OK to open the curtains. I still try to take the first shower of the day because if Karen goes ahead of me, I come out of the shower to find her standing by the window with one hand on the curtains.

She waits about five seconds then asks, "Is it OK if I open them now?"

"Does it look OK?" Is always my response.

"I don't know. How would I know?"

"You would know by looking at me and seeing if I'm dressed yet."

"You look dressed to me."

"I only have a shirt on. I'm not wearing pants. Is that dressed?"

"You look fine. I'm opening the curtains."

"Nope. Remember? We have a truce."

"OK, but come on! It's a beautiful day!"

I sense it's a fragile truce and I live with the fear that someday I'll walk out of the bathroom with a towel around my waist and she'll be standing there with the door open to the hallway saying, "Hey, I'm going to get more coffee do you want any?"

"No, please shut the door!"

"How about some yogurt?"

"No!"

"Cereal?"

"No!"

"Sliced ham?"

She would do this, and I think she is waiting for just the right moment.

YELLOWSTONE AND GRAND TETON

The plan for the week was to spend a couple of nights in Gardiner, Montana and visit Yellowstone National Park. From there we would drive to Grand Teton National Park and share a Colter Bay cabin for one night. The following two nights we rented a house in Moab, and then we'd drive from Moab to Flagstaff.

Our drive from Missoula to Gardiner took about four hours. Gardiner is on the northern border of Yellowstone and about five miles north of Mammoth Hot Springs. It's been the northern gateway to the park for as long as the park has existed. In 1903, an arch was built to serve as the official north entrance. Teddy Roosevelt was visiting the park during the arch's construction, and they asked him to lay the cornerstone. Now named the Roosevelt Arch, it's just south of town, and you drive through it on your way into the park.

We arrived at our motel just after noon. I'd guess it had about seventy-five rooms, but the parking lot was empty. We weren't sure they were open until we went to the front desk inside the lobby. The person working the reception desk told us our room was ready so we could check in early. John asked, "Do you have a lot of vacancies? The parking lot is empty.

"No, sir. We're totally booked for the week. No rooms

available."

"Then everyone must be in the park?"

"Yeah, we have a lot of tour groups stay here. They come in buses at the end of the day and leave early each morning."

The four of us shared a two-bedroom suite with a kitchen. Both Lolly and Karen each brought with them enough groceries to feed all of us for the entire week. They busied themselves by putting away the groceries and settling in.

John and I stood watching as they nested. "We're only going to be here two nights," we both said at the same time.

"Let's grab a quick lunch and go into the park. We have enough time to do a hike," I suggested.

"Alright then, we'll make sandwiches."

Karen and Lolly proceeded to open, unwrap, and unpackage nearly every food item they'd brought, then formed an assembly line. John gave me a look that said, "We might want to sit down. This could take awhile." It took several tries, but we got Karen and Lolly loaded into John's truck before the afternoon got away from us. We were all a bit car-weary from the 700-mile drive from Seattle and wanted to stretch our legs in the park. I was also hoping to see wildlife, maybe a bear.

A few weeks before, I'd put my canister of bear spray in my to-go pile so we would have it for hiking in Yellowstone and Grand Teton National Parks. One fact had been nagging at me: it was past its expiration date, a couple of years past. I realize bear spray doesn't stay useable forever, but it's not cheap. I thought, "Do I really need to get a new one?"

Finally, I decided that it would be cheaper to buy a new canister of bear spray than pay for years of plastic surgery to reconstruct my face after a bear chews it off. Time was running out though, the trip date was near, so Karen and I headed to REI for "a few last items," and a fresh bear spray.

We were fortunate that REI had it in stock; often they are sold out. I was standing in front of the display still not sure I needed a new one. Karen had seen this scenario play out before, many times. She'd watched me take the bear spray off the shelf, then put it back, then take it off the shelf again, and then put it back again. She knew if she didn't intervene I'd spend the rest of the afternoon doing this.

"Just buy it so we can go," she said.

"How can bear spray expire? Does it start to smell bad?" I asked.

"Maybe when it gets old it doesn't shoot as forcefully as it could before," she said with a giggle. "You know, weak stream."

"We're still talking about the bear spray, right?" I replied.

"Or, maybe it loses its spiciness when it gets old." More giggling.

"Still bear spray, correct?"

"What do you think I'm talking about?"

"Pepper doesn't lose its spiciness," I replied confidently without a clue if my statement was correct. The "not shooting forcefully" comment worried me though.

And how would I know if it wasn't "shooting as forcefully as before"? I'd never shot my bear spray. Once I seriously considered spraying it on the moles that destroy our backyard, but Karen intervened. The fact remained, I'd never shot it before, and this concerned me.

I became genuinely worried after I thought about it more. If we came across a bear in the wild that wanted to mess with us, I'd first need to read the label to be confident I was shooting the bear spray correctly. Not only would this require an uninterrupted moment of peace and quiet, but first I'd have to find my reading glasses and proper lighting.

The closest I've come to practicing was removing the safety from the trigger one night while lying in bed. I keep the bear spray on the nightstand by my side of the bed to protect against burglars. Taking the safety off scared me a little, but putting it back on was even scarier. I almost sprayed Karen by accident while she was sleeping.

Finally, the doubt Karen put in my brain about the expired bear spray convinced me to buy a new one. I also vowed to practice before our trip. "The moles won't know what hit 'em," I said to Karen as we drove home.

"You're not shooting the moles with bear spray," she said calmly. "Our granddaughter plays back there."

I didn't respond. If there is one thing I've learned in thirty-four years of marriage it's that not everything said requires a response. But I thought to myself, "If a man cannot shoot moles with bear spray in his backyard is he indeed a man?" It didn't matter. I had forgotten about the moles before we arrived home. With an endless list of to-dos that needed doing before the trip, I never thought about the bear spray again after I placed it in my duffel bag. That's not entirely accurate. I did think about it again, as we were talking with the ranger in the visitor center at Yellowstone. That's when I remembered that my bear spray was still in my duffel bag, which was sitting on the bed in our motel room—in Gardiner.

At the visitor center, we had a nice, long chat with the ranger about which hike we should do that afternoon. By "we" I mean Karen. She likes to be the one to ask the rangers questions. We (Karen) decided that the Bunsen Peak Trail a few miles south of the Mammoth Hot Springs area was the best choice.

"Oh yeah, one last question," Karen said to the ranger. "Do we *need* bear spray for this hike?"

"Of course you do! You must have bear spray with you when you hike in the park," was his reply.

"Even for Bunsen Peak? It's just off the road. We won't be in the *wilderness* wilderness; we'll be able to see the road from the trail."

"Yes, ma'am! Hikers should be prepared to encounter bears on any of the trails in the park."

There was no mistaking his advice. He didn't say it was a good idea to carry bear spray. He didn't say you might want to think about carrying bear spray. He said, "You must."

In 2016, the National Park Service reported that the grizzly population in the Greater Yellowstone Ecosystem was estimated to be 690, plus an unknown number of black bears.

Since 1980, there have been thirty-four reports of human injuries caused by grizzlies in the park, an average of about one per year. Almost all of those injuries occurred in the backcountry. While that might seem small considering the number of bears in the area and the vast numbers of people who visit the park each year, the threat is real. In separate, unrelated incidents in 2011 and 2015, grizzly bears killed three hikers in the park; none of them were carrying bear spray.

We were lucky that the visitor center bookstore sold bear spray, and that John was planning on purchasing one anyway. With John now packing we didn't need to take a detour back to Gardiner before driving to the trailhead.

Bunsen Peak Trail is a moderately strenuous, four-mile loop hike with about 1,300 feet of elevation gain. The weather changed continuously as we trudged up the trail. One moment the sun shone brightly, and the next, dark clouds threatened to soak us. The one aspect of the weather that didn't change the entire time was the wind. It howled. The temperature was in the 50s, but it felt much colder. The wind penetrated my raincoat as if it were a loosely knit sweater and sucked the heat right out of me. Regardless, it was good to get exercise after driving for a day and a half, and the views from the top were amazing. And no bear encounters. Our only wildlife sighting was a lone mountain goat on the back side of Bunsen Peak.

Despite our concern about bear encounters, I had to laugh as the wind nearly blew us off the mountain. Had we run across a bear and needed to use bear spray, I'm not sure we could have safely done so in the strong, shifting wind. One of the few things I can think of worse than having to negotiate with an enraged grizzly at close range would be to shoot bear spray at it and have the spray blow back in my face. That would be like saying to the bear, "You win, I give up, you can eat me now, and by the way, I've seasoned myself so enjoy." Then, while you stumble blindly through the woods coughing up a gallbladder, the bear can take its time eating you at his or her leisure. Yep, you need to be careful using bear spray on a windy day.

When we were back at the motel, I was curious what bear spray experts recommend in windy conditions. I found a couple of useful videos online. I learned a lot, including that the best you can do if you are downwind from a bear and it charges, is to try to at least position yourself crosswind from the bear, so the spray doesn't come back at you.

The video described the ideal way to use bear spray to deter an attack. First, if the bear is not aggressive, like charging you, you are better off remaining calm while trying to back out of the area. If the bear does charge, you are supposed to shoot the spray at the charging bear when it's about 10-15 yards away so that it passes through the cloud of spray on its path to you. But what if you are shaking so hard (and most likely soiling yourself at the same moment) that your aim is slightly off? Or, way off? And here's a key question: what if the bear doesn't pass through the cloud of spray? It's not like obedience school for bears. You can't withhold the treat, grab him by the ear, march him back fifteen yards and say, "Let's try that again." No, at that point, you're a bear toy. You wouldn't even have time to run, which you shouldn't do anyway, but trust me, you'll run—if you haven't passed out from fear. (Yeah, this is something I need to practice. More about that in a minute.) Still, your chances of survival are much better if you carry the spray than if you don't.

Another interesting fact I learned from the video was that the product might fail to discharge at temperatures below freezing. Good to know. Or, at the other extreme, the canister might explode—yes explode—at temperatures above 120 degrees. For this reason, the manufacturer recommends not transporting bear spray inside the passenger compartment of a vehicle. When outside temperatures range from 80-100, the temperature inside a vehicle can climb to 130-172 degrees. Imagine opening your car door on a hot day to find your bear spray had spontaneously discharged while you were away. That's going to hurt your trade-in value.

Toward the end of the video, an image came on the screen that startled me. It was an outdoor setting with two people standing next to a tent. A man was pointing a bear spray canister at a woman, who appeared to be his female camping partner. She had her back turned to him and her hands in the air. The image had a large circle with an X through the middle indicating, "Don't do this!"

At first, I thought they were warning not to use bear spray to settle domestic disputes. Instead, they were instructing the viewer to not use bear spray in the same manner as bug spray. In other words, don't spray it on yourself thinking this will repel bears the same way bug spray repels insects. (I couldn't make this stuff up.) I have to believe that the producers of the video added this pearl of wisdom because people have tried this in the past. Now, I don't want to sound supercilious, again, but wouldn't you think a product that has a *safety* on the *trigger* would cause the user to pause and wonder, "Hmmm, this looks a little different than that Backwoods Off! I just put on, maybe I should read the label?"

Come to think of it, spraying yourself with bear spray is 100% effective at preventing bear attacks. Not that it keeps bears away, but because there has never been a bear attack inside a hospital emergency room, which is where you'd be spending the next day or two.

The final recommendation was to practice spraying before you go into the wilderness. Yes! I made Karen watch that part of the video.

"You see? I have a responsibility for our safety that requires I practice," I said to her.

"You are not practicing on the moles in our backyard," was all she said.

After the hike in the park and a quick dinner in town, we went back to our motel room and played cards. Outside our room was a wide porch with a picnic table centered in front of the door of our room and the two rooms next to ours. It was a community space for all the guests to share. Without the wind blowing on us, the temperature was mild enough for us to sit outside in shirtsleeves and still be comfortable. It was getting late and the sun was down, but there still weren't many cars in the parking lot.

We watched as tour buses pulled into the empty lot and weary travelers staggered off. Each bus had a tour guide with a clipboard and sets of keys. As people got off the bus, the guide told them their room numbers and handed them their keys. They grabbed their luggage and headed toward their rooms.

Two young men walked by us and unlocked the door right next to ours. They weren't in their room but a couple of minutes and they left, meeting two young women in the parking lot, and walking into town together. About an hour later they came back with bags of carryout food. We were still playing cards at the picnic table.

When they passed us again, we said hello and asked them what they had done that day. Their English was hard to understand, but we were able to get most of it. They also told us where they were from and their itinerary for the week. It sounded like a lot of time on a bus. They had flown from China to San Francisco, started the tour there, and rode a bus to Yellowstone. Lolly asked them what they were doing the next day. One of the women answered by saying they didn't know, that they would find out in the morning. Lolly thought the woman said as she pointed to the parking lot, "The tall guy tells us each day what the plan is."

Lolly looked back at the parking lot where the tour buses were parked, and then responded, "Oh, I see. The tall guy has the schedule and lets you know each day where you're going?" The woman looked confused. Lolly kept talking, "We should have a tall guy who plans everything for us. You just get up each day and ask the tall guy what's next." Karen, John and I were giving Lolly wide-eyed looks, as if to say, "Stop talking!" But she kept going; tall guy this and tall guy that.

Once we said goodnight to our new friends and they went

into their room, John said to Lolly, "She said, 'tour guide' not 'tall guy.' What is wrong with you?"

For the rest of the week, we worked the words "tall guy" into every conversation possible. You don't want to make a mistake like that when traveling with us, especially early in the trip.

In the morning, the four of us went in John's truck to the Old Faithful Visitor Center in the park. John and Lolly had never seen Old Faithful Geyser. It took us an extra hour to get there because the National Park Service had closed one of the main roads for maintenance. Karen spent the entire drive describing how spectacular the sight of Old Faithful is when it erupts.

Sometimes she gets excited and over-sells. She also can be a jinx. In fact, one of her many nicknames is Jinxy Jinxter. I wasn't too surprised when we got to Old Faithful, missed the last eruption by four minutes, walked all of the boardwalks around the small geysers, twice, finally stood there to watch Old Faithful blow, and got a dud eruption. It just sputtered.

We learned at the Visitor Center that if an eruption lasts less than two and a half minutes, then it's likely to be a sixty-minute interval before the next eruption. If the eruption lasts longer than two and a half minutes, the interval is likely to be ninety minutes. There was no way we were staying for a 62ish-minute wait to see the next eruption, so we went for a hike. A ranger recommended Mystic Falls and Biscuit Basin Overlook, which took us to the top of a clearing that overlooked Old Faithful from two miles away.

The group had no trouble talking me into doing the hike. As soon as I heard "biscuit," I was in. I love biscuits. Many times Karen and I have chosen hikes solely because of the name. Karen is a sucker for any trail with the word "sugar" in its name. They could make a path to the top of a radioactive medical waste landfill and if they named it Sugarloaf Mountain Trail, she would insist we hike it.

When we got to the overlook, I was able to get a cell signal on my phone, so I looked up the next eruption time on the

Internet. It was a few minutes away. This time, even from far away, the eruption was spectacular, just as Karen had described earlier. The jinx was off.

Over the course of our two days in Yellowstone, we saw a black bear with cubs, a brown bear (a real brown bear, not a black bear that was brown), mountain goat, bighorn sheep, wolf, bison, elk, and deer. That's a good list of large mammals to have seen in a couple of days, except we didn't see a moose. The moose sighting happened the following day in Grand Teton National Park.

Inspiration Point was the destination of our hike in Grand Teton NP. At the point where the trail around Jenny Lake turns up toward Cascade Canyon and begins to gain elevation, we came across a group of people who were standing off to the side of the trail looking into the forest. A mother moose and her two calves were feeding on leaves surprisingly close to where the onlookers were standing—maybe thirty yards away. She must have been accustomed to humans otherwise she wouldn't have let her babies feed there. A few years earlier, Karen and I saw a moose very close to that same area of the park.

The mother and babies were calm, and the hikers gave her plenty of space. The four of us continued up the trail to Inspiration Point, took pictures, and then hiked further up the canyon. The leaves of the deciduous trees and bushes were in full color. We hated to turn around, but every step took us further from where we'd parked, and we wanted to make it back to the truck before dark.

MOAB

It took us almost eleven hours the next day to drive from Colter Bay Village in Grand Teton NP to Moab, Utah. There were several areas along our drive I would have liked to stop and explore, places we'd never seen before: Flaming Gorge National Recreation Area, Ashley National Forest, and Dinosaur National Monument. But the drive was already too long, so we bookmarked them in our minds to visit another time.

None of the hotels in Moab had vacancies when we planned our trip. Lolly found a house online that was large enough for the four of us to share. The location was very convenient, a couple of blocks away from the town's main street. It was a great place to make our home base while we explored the area.

On our first full day in Moab, we went into Arches National Park. Since John and Lolly hadn't been there before, we wanted to show them the highlights. Delicate Arch was our first stop of the day.

The weather was perfect, which guaranteed that crowds of people would be on the trail. Despite the number of hikers, our run of wildlife sightings continued as we hiked toward the arch. We saw a small animal scamper across the path about thirty feet in front of us. It looked like a miniature coyote with big ears. I was able to keep it in sight for a couple of minutes before it disappeared into the desert. Later we learned it was a kit fox.

At the end of the trail was what some say is the most photographed sight in Utah: Delicate Arch. Whenever I see a photo of Delicate Arch, my mind draws a crowd of people just outside the frame of the picture. Rarely is the area around the arch not crowded, and people usually form a line to wait for a turn to have their photo taken under the arch. I've gotten over being frustrated with the crowds at popular sites in national parks, but I still scratch my head at the poses people strike when it's their turn. I appreciate an imaginary lightsaber battle routine as much as the next guy, but do you have to video it three times while dozens of other people are waiting?

The four of us stood in just the right spot to get a photo of the arch, but it was impossible to catch a moment when there weren't people walking through the scene. This is a common problem during spring, summer, and fall. On our last trip, a woman sat down in the middle of the arch's opening, took a paper sack out of her backpack, and proceeded to eat her lunch.

It was quickly apparent to John and I that we wouldn't get a clean shot of the arch, so we went off to explore the area off to the side of the arch where there were fewer people. We were about a hundred yards away, looking at the view to the east when we heard a woman's voice yell, "Hey, people! Could everyone please step away from the arch for a minute so the rest of us can take a picture without anyone in it?" John looked at me and said, "That voice sounded familiar," I said, "Yep, that's my gal." Karen had assumed crowd control authority back at the arch. John and I walked back in time to see Karen and Lolly directing people away from the arch. It was like Moses parting the sea. They were motioning with their hands as if to say, "Back! Back it up some more. You over there, a little to the left, move it!" As soon as the area was clear, you could hear the sound of cameras clicking from all directions.

John and I started hiking toward the truck without making eye contact with Karen and Lolly. I said to him, "Don't look at them and no one will know they're with us."

We were hoping we'd see the miniature coyote again, but we didn't. Nothing makes a hike memorable like a good wildlife sighting. It was mid-day by the time we finished the Delicate Arch hike, so we drove to the parking lot of Devil's Garden, and ate lunch on the tailgate of John's truck. Devil's Garden contains the largest concentration of natural arches in the world. It's very popular, and there are usually masses of people on the trail. But as it is with many hikes in the national parks, once you get a mile or so down the trail, you're usually pretty much alone. Two miles from the trailhead is a spot to view Double O Arch. Just beyond this is the beginning of the Primitive Trail. The trail is marked with a warning sign that says, "Caution – Primitive Trail – Difficult Hiking." It's at this point where many hikers turn back and retrace their steps to the parking lot.

The more adventurous keep going. There are a few places along the trail where it can be tricky to figure out if you're still on the correct path, especially if there aren't other hikers around. At one point the trail leads up and across a narrow rock fin that has drop-offs on both sides high enough that you would be seriously injured or killed if you fell off. Karen and I had walked across that fin before, on a previous visit to the park, when the wind was gusting. That was a scary moment, but we managed to make it to the other side without incident.

This time, when we got to the same fin, John and Lolly were behind us taking pictures. Karen and I were halfway across when we noticed three women on a tiny ledge trying to scale the side of the fin. They must have missed the markers at the far side that indicate how to get on top. By the time we saw them and asked if they needed help, they had gotten themselves stuck. They couldn't pull themselves up to the top of the fin and couldn't turn back. I told them to stay where they were. It made me very nervous seeing them on that ledge. If any of them had slipped they would have fallen at least thirty feet onto the rocks below.

I crouched down and leaned over the side of the fin. Karen held onto my left arm and I extended my right arm down to the woman closest to me. It took all of Karen's and my weight to pull her to the top of the fin. Then I did the same for the other two. The women looked to be about the same age as our daughters. I had to stop myself from lecturing them to be more careful.

John and Lolly caught up with us after the women thanked us and hiked off. "What was that?" John asked. "Are you stopping to give all the young ladies a hand up now?"

"They were trapped," I replied.

"They didn't look trapped to me. They looked like they were trying to get away from the creepy, old guy on the trail when they passed us," John said.

"Don't say that about yourself. You're not a creepy, old guy, John. You're just old," I said.

A mile or so along the trail, we stopped on an outcropping of slick rock to rest and eat a snack (second lunch) while looking at the expansive views of the park. I could have taken a nap on the smooth, warm rock, but the others were restless to keep going. The hike back was much less crowded until the Primitive Trail rejoined the main trail. Then it was a matter of snaking our way through the crowd of visitors back to the truck.

We spent the rest of the afternoon poking around the local attractions. We all were a bit weary after the hikes, and John was sure that the 190-million-year-old dinosaur footprints we showed him off State Road 279 just west of town were fakes. "That? You think that's a dinosaur footprint? Some local probably carved that last week. Look, it only has three toes." He wasn't much more impressed with the petroglyphs we stopped to look at either. John's reaction was a sure sign it was time to call it a day.

Back at the Moab house, we had a period of quiet time. I

took a short nap then inventoried the gear and clothing I was planning to take on the trip down the Colorado River. I spread everything I had brought on the floor, couches, and chairs of the family room. It was a lot of stuff, too much I thought.

When we got the O.A.R.S. suggested packing list in the mail, I felt I would be in good shape drawing from my existing stock of clothes, gear, and gadgets. Most items made sense: swim trunks, sunscreen and extra hiking socks. Others were confusing: whiskbroom (it was confusing as to why this was on the list until we got up the first morning and couldn't clean the sand off our tarp or the floor of our tent to save our lives), and feminine urinary device (I still don't know what this is).

I had to buy a couple of things though. I needed to replace my tiny roll of duct tape that I had taken on every trip in the last ten years. You don't want to go into the wilderness with a stale roll of duct tape; that would be foolish.

Camp towel. A quick-drying camp towel was on the list. What I would need to dry I wasn't sure, but O.A.R.S. suggested we each have one so I bought a camp towel. Two, in fact, a small one and a large one. I had to buy the large towel twice. Months before the trip, I purchased my camp towels at REI and put them on the chair in the corner of our bedroom, which was the temporary home for my trip pile. (My trip things were on a different chair in a different corner of our bedroom than Karen's fashion show pile. It's essential for the longevity of our marriage that these piles don't touch.) A couple of weeks before our departure, Karen was eyeing my pile. She was inspecting it from a safe distance as if she were examining a large cactus. She asked, "Where's your large towel?"

"Right here," I said, holding the unopened package out so she could get a good look at it.

"Oh, honey, that's not nearly large enough," was her reply. She never calls me "honey."

"Large enough for what?"

"What do you think the towel is for?" she asked.

"Drying–stuff," I said.

"It's for drying off after you bathe in the river. Take it out of the package and let's see how big it is," she said.

I took it out and tried to unfold it. I soon realized it was already unfolded.

"Wrap it around your waist. Let's see how it looks," she said.

When I tried, the corners of the towel—the long way— did not touch. There was at least a six-inch gap between the ends. Karen laughed so hard she cried. For the next week all I had to do was hold up the towel, and she would start crying. I got a bigger one before the trip.

Now that we were in Moab and only a couple of days away from the start of the river trip, I began to doubt that I would have the nerve to bathe in the Colorado River. I searched the Internet and read that water coming out of the Glen Canyon Dam is between 48 and 55 degrees year round. John had been ribbing me every night while we played cards. He kept saying, "I can't wait to see you two take a bath in the Colorado River." He would follow with a hearty belly laugh and a sip of whiskey. Lolly was no better. John's remark always sent her leaning out of her chair laughing.

I became resolute after the first couple of nights of his taunting that we would brave the cold and prove him wrong. But then my doubt began to grow. What if John was right? What if the river was crazy cold? What if my soft, white underbelly couldn't take the frigid temperature? What if...? It made sense to have a plan B.

That night when we played cards, I asked John, "OK, fine. How do you plan on staying clean on the river?"

Lolly disappeared into the adjoining bedroom then reappeared with a Costco-sized package of adult wipes. "Here, we'll share," she said.

The side of the package read, "Cleaning, Bathing, Sanitation, 12 inches by 8 inches."

"Those are huge! Is your plan to whip these out and clean,

bathe and sanitize while we all sit around the campfire?" I asked.

"They *are* bigger than I thought they'd be, but no, we'll do our business in our tent."

"I'm not sure I want to wipe my entire body down with those things. They probably leave you sticky," I said. I don't like being sticky, who does?

John rejoined the conversation, "You don't wipe everything, just your crotal area."

"My what?" I asked. Karen had her face buried in her hands.

"Trust me. I've been on a lot of fishing trips in Alaska where there's nowhere to bathe. All you need are wet wipes. The key is to keep your crotal area clean. Keep your crotal area clean, and you have nothing to worry about."

Maybe it was the whiskey we were drinking, or maybe I was trying hard to convince myself that anything was better than freezing to death in the river, but this made complete sense. It was a perfect plan B. Heck, it was a perfect plan A. "Keep your crotal area clean, and you have nothing to worry about." Those are words to live by. Although, *crotal* isn't a word.

As generous as Lolly's offer was to share her wipes, we thought it best to get our own. Besides, I couldn't envision how the "sharing" would go. Was I supposed to try and catch her attention once a day when the other twenty-four people weren't around and ask, "Hey, Lolly, uh, could I, uh, you know, could I have another crotal wipe?"

The next morning Karen and I went to a drug store in Moab. We both knew what we were there to do, but we didn't talk about it. Karen went immediately to the live bait section of the store and acted like she wasn't with me. I had no problem shopping for adult wipes. I was looking for a store employee to show me where they were when I stumbled across them next to the adult diapers. I was pleased to find a package of wipes that were much smaller than Lolly's. They were eight inches by six inches, just right for the river. I collected Karen and went to the front of the store to check out. I paid, then the cashier put the wipes in a bag and handed it to me. I turned toward Karen, but she was gone.

"Where'd she go?"

The cashier said, "She just left. It looked like she was in a hurry."

I nodded understandingly at the cashier then glanced at the bag of wipes. My look said it all, "Yeah, why do you think we need these?"

The drugstore was our last stop in Moab. We were anxious to get on the road. It was hard to believe that in less than twenty-four hours we would be on our way to the Colorado River.

Delicate Arch, Arches National Park

FLAGSTAFF

About a hundred miles south of Moab we turned onto Highway 163. A few miles past the town of Mexican Hat we entered the Navajo Reservation. In Utah, Monument Valley is on Navajo land. Just as the rock formations come into view, there's a section of highway where cars are always parked on the shoulder, and people are standing in the road. It's where they shot a famous scene from the movie *Forrest Gump*. The scene where Forrest decides to stop running and go home was filmed with the monuments in the background. It's a cool spot to take a picture, but a little dangerous when there's traffic. The problem is, to get the perfect shot you need to stand in the middle of the road, which makes for an unsafe situation if either the passing drivers or the person standing in the road aren't paying close attention. We've seen some strange things there before: people dressed up like Forrest Gump, people doing handstands in the middle of the road, and skateboarders trying to get a picture of themselves while skating down the center of the highway.

Just past Monument Valley, the skies opened, and we drove through heavy rain almost the entire rest of the way to Flagstaff. The rain seemed like a bad omen, but we kept our spirits up thinking about the trip.

It was too early to check into the DoubleTree Hotel when

we got to Flagstaff, so we headed to Lumberyard Brewing Company to have lunch with several of the other couples who had also just arrived. We were like children on Christmas Eve, we just wanted it to be the next day.

Having had only John and Lolly to talk to about the river trip all week, I wanted to get the others' opinions on a few things.

"By a show of hands, how many of you brought a camp towel with you?" Everyone's hand went up.

"How many of you plan on bathing in the river?" Again, it was unanimous.

"Final question, how many of you brought adult wipes?" No hands went up. All I got were confused looks.

"See John, what do you know?"

John shook his head and stood his ground. "We'll just see how many of you bathe in the river. You'll come out of the river dirtier than you went in."

That evening we gathered in a room off the lobby of the DoubleTree for an orientation with our trip leader. One of the reasons the tour company requires passengers to attend a meeting the night before is to make sure everyone made it to Flagstaff and is ready to leave the next morning. At seven o'clock sharp we were all present.

Our trip leader, Eric, lives in Whitefish, Montana. He explained to us that many of the O.A.R.S. boatmen contract one or two trips a year in the Grand Canyon. He was tall and athletic, and his white hair and beard gave him the look of a thinner and younger version of Martin Litton, the iconic boatman whose advocacy for protecting wild places is legendary. Eric was also a boatman; he piloted the lead dory on our trip. It was clear that he took his responsibility for leading our group seriously, yet he had a calm and stoic demeanor. His engaging smile and mannerisms put us all at ease right away. Eric was relaxed and he spoke as if he was already on river time. Despite the fluorescent lighting and carpet of the conference room, I could imagine us all being around a campfire together. Twenty-four hours later we were.

At these meetings, the passengers often meet each other for the first time and become somewhat familiar before they launch into the wilderness together. Eric asked us to introduce ourselves and say how we knew each other. Since we were mostly well acquainted beforehand, that part of the meeting went quickly.

Besides Karen and I, there were seven other couples in our group.

Craig and Aya, from Seattle. Craig and I worked together years ago and the four of us have remained friends ever since. Without his initiative to research the guide companies and make the reservation, the trip wouldn't have happened.

John and Lolly, from the Seattle area. Karen and Lolly worked together many years ago along with Sue, of *Dear Bob and Sue* fame. We've traveled many times together with John and Lolly, and continue to do so.

Phill (yes, that's correct, he has two l's in his first name) and Wendy, also from Seattle, and also a former co-worker of mine, along with Craig. We've remained close friends with them over the years.

Mark and Rachel, from the Seattle area. We didn't know them before the trip. Mark and Phill have known each other since junior high. Mark and Rachel joined our group at the last minute when our friends Steve and Cindy had to cancel.

Bart and his wife Joe, from Utah. We'd met them twice before the trip. They used to live in Seattle and were originally friends of Craig and Aya.

Paul and Debi, from Portland, Oregon. We hadn't met them before the trip. They're long-time friends of Craig and Aya.

Iain and Gill (short for Gillian), from Toronto. Like Paul and Debi, they're long-time friends of Craig and Aya. We'd met them once before the trip.

The orientation was Eric's opportunity to tell us what to expect during the trip and to provide a few guidelines. "If you have any food you want to bring, give it to me, and I'll put it in my dory. If you store it in your dry bag, rodents will sniff it out and chew through your bag to get to it. Also, if you are bringing alcohol in addition to what you ordered, give that to me as well so I can keep it in my dory. You're welcome to drink it when we are in camp, but you can't drink alcohol when we are on the river."

Most of what Eric told us we'd read in the O.A.R.S. literature before the trip. His job that night was more about getting to know us and determine how much of a pain in the ass we would be on the river. Also, he was there to give us our dry bags, which we would have to pack before the next morning.

O.A.R.S. provided each of us with two dry bags, one for all of our clothes and gear that would be packed away each day while we were on the river, and a second smaller bag for any personal items we wanted access to during the day while on the boats. When sealed correctly, these bags keep whatever is in them dry regardless of how wet the outside gets. You could throw your bag in the river, fish it out and your stuff would still be dry—if you sealed it correctly.

On this trip, there was a third dry bag that held our sleeping kits. Each contained a sleeping bag with a liner, a pillow with a pillowcase, and a tarp. All sixteen of us chose to rent a sleeping kit from O.A.R.S. You are not required to rent the kit from them, but it was much easier than bringing our own.

Eric dumped the dry bags in the center of the room and instructed us to grab a big one and a little one. Every bag had a number written on the side. Our job was to remember our bag's number so we could tell which one was ours at the end of each day. The sleep kit bags were also numbered. Every night we would use the same sleep kit, the one whose number matched the number on our dry bag.

Since there were no more questions, we were free to go. "Let's start gathering here in the lobby tomorrow morning about 6:00 am. We want to be packed and ready to pull out of the parking lot at 6:30," he said. Karen and I chose our bags, said goodnight to the group and went off to pack.

Having driven down to Flagstaff, we had the luxury of bringing with us just about every piece of gear and clothing we *might* want to take with us on the river. This only delayed the inevitable. We now had to take our large piles of stuff and make smaller piles that would fit into the dry bags.

Karen and I had a room with two queen beds, so we each had plenty of space to organize and pack. While Karen was doing one last fashion show, I laid everything I had intended to take on my bed. For what seemed like an uncomfortable amount of time I would look at the pile on the bed, look at the dry bags, and repeat. I could tell without trying to fill the bags that it wouldn't all fit. It was getting late, so I quickly went through all of my stuff one last time and reduced my pile by about a third. I no longer had time to obsess over each item. I needed to get my bags packed and get to bed so I would have a chance at a restful night of sleep.

As O.A.R.S. had advised, we'd packed our clothes in large freezer bags: socks in one, long johns in another, a couple of t-shirts per bag, etc. This served several purposes: it would make it easier to find an article of clothing later, it allowed us to keep clean and dirty clothes separated, and in case we hadn't properly sealed our dry bags our clothes would have a second layer of protection from getting wet.

I first put all of my clothes in Ziploc bags before testing whether they would fit into the dry bag. There is a trick to compressing the dry bag so all the air comes out while also sealing it tight so no water can get in. If you try to seal it too early, you can't compress the air out of the bag so that everything fits. With a few tries, I figured out the right combination of pushes and pulls that worked. But I quickly learned a flaw to the freezer bag system. Each of the bags still had a little bit of air in them that prevented them from being compressed further once in the dry bag. I had to remove all the freezer bags and squeeze every last bit of air out of each one before sealing them, so they were nice and compact. Now with all of my freezer bags sprawled across the bed, I began re-packing the dry bag. As I was placing them in the dry bag, I realized I couldn't tell what was in each freezer bag. The freezer bags were clear of course, but my clothes were all very similar in color. Once compressed I couldn't tell my underwear from my t-shirts from my long johns. This may not seem like a huge problem at first, but when it's bedtime and dark on the sandy beach, and the temperature is dropping rapidly, it's nice to be able to quickly find your fleece pullover in your dry bag. With your head and headlamp down inside your dry bag, it's almost impossible to tell what's in each bag, especially with the glare of the headlamp on the freezer bags.

A simple solution to this would have been to label each bag with a Sharpie. It was fortunate that I had prepared so thoroughly that I had a Sharpie with me on the trip, but I couldn't find it. I had so much stuff I couldn't find anything when I needed it. The lesson: it's not whether you *have* the thing you need, it's whether you can *find* it when you need it. I was drowning in stuff. Karen calls this being overprepared, a state that I denied was possible until twenty minutes later when I had to give up my search for the Sharpie. Evil Sharpie!

That night I slept for two hours at the most, finally getting out of bed at 5:00 am. There was no use lying there any longer. My OC got the better of me, and I grabbed a couple of additional items that I was sure I would need on the river. It was dark in our room, and Karen was still sleeping. When I opened my large dry bag, it filled the room with light. My headlamp had been on all night inside the bag. When I had compressed the bag the night before, the pressure on the on/off switch must have caused the light to turn on. It was a good thing I saw this. I grabbed extra batteries for my headlamp and tossed them in as well.

Highway 163 approaching Monument Valley from the north.
Location of the scene from the movie *Forrest Gump*.

LAUNCH

At 6:00 am, Karen and I had loaded our luggage onto a cart and headed toward the lobby. We thought we might be first to get there, but when we arrived nearly all of the other couples were ready to go. It was sunny, but the temperature was chilly that morning in Flagstaff. I was still dressed for fall weather, but the rest of the group was wearing summer outfits. I had a hard time imagining that in a few hours we'd be standing on the banks of the Colorado River in shorts and t-shirts. The elevation of Flagstaff is about 6,900 feet; Lees Ferry, where we would enter the river, is 3,200 feet. That's almost two-thirds of a mile difference in elevation. By the time we got to Lees Ferry, we'd be back in summer.

There was a lot of nervous conversation while we waited for the vans to arrive. I went over to Phill and asked him where his dry bags were. "Right there," he said pointing. A few feet away sat a large dry bag that was half the size of mine. Phill's bag was sealed shut but there was plenty of extra room left inside.

"That's what you're bringing for the entire week?" I asked.

"Yeah, I'm not sure I'll need all of it though."

"Are you going to wear what you have on right now all week?" I asked.

"Matt, we're going on a float trip. You should relax. I

83

promise you won't smell me all week," he responded.

"You're right. Maybe I need to take some stuff out of my bag."

"By the way, why do you have winter clothes on?" Phill asked.

"I have my boat clothes on underneath," I said.

"This week is going to be good for you. It'll help you unwind," he replied.

The last thing we did before loading the vans was put our extra luggage into a storage room that the DoubleTree had reserved for O.A.R.S. Just before 6:30 am, two vans pulled into the parking lot, each towing a trailer with a dory on top. It was then we got our first look at the boats we would be riding in all week. They were clean and shiny as if they were ready for their maiden voyage. What's probably more likely is they had just come off the river a couple of days before and rushed back to Flagstaff for a good scrubbing before our trip.

One of the dories was named *Black Canyon*; it belonged to Andre, a boatman on our trip. The other had *Marble Canyon* painted on its side. Several of us gathered around the *Marble Canyon*; we were staring at it with awe. Someone said, "Do you think it's OK to touch it?" It looked like a museum piece. A movie that many of us had watched, about this very boat, was fueling our excitement. *Martin's Boat* is a video documentary about the building of the dory *Marble Canyon* as a tribute to Martin Litton, and its maiden voyage in 2015.

Someone could write an entire book about Martin Litton's life; he was a remarkable man. Martin founded the guide company Grand Canyon Dories that's now part of the O.A.R.S. group of companies, and he rallied the cause for stopping the construction of Marble Canyon Dam, which—had it been built—would have flooded forty miles of the Grand Canyon. The movie *Martin's Boat* can be found online. It provides a primer about Martin. The Winter 2014-2015 issue of the *boatman's quarterly review* (volume 28 number 1) also has a lengthy article about Martin's life. I was able to find a copy of this issue online as well. Martin Litton died in 2014 at the age of ninety-seven.

As fragile as these boats look out of the water, they're capable of carrying five people and a large amount of cargo through the canyon. Their wooden hulls are more susceptible to damage from rocks and debris than rubber rafts, but in comparison, dories are much more maneuverable. A skilled boatman has a better chance of avoiding obstacles on the river in a dory than in a lumbering raft. When Martin Litton started his river guiding company in 1962, he insisted on using wooden drift boats. He called them dories because they resembled New England fishing dories. Litton had a tradition of naming his dories after wild places that were lost, compromised or threatened by human development.

It would have been much easier for him to run the river in the rubber rafts that were becoming available to the public once the military began selling their surplus. But wooden boats provided passengers—and boatmen—a more intimate trip down the river, something closer to what John Wesley Powell experienced on his expeditions. (In 1869, Powell led a three-month river expedition from Green River Station, Wyoming to the confluence of the Colorado and Virgin Rivers. As part of that journey, Powell and crew became the first group to explore the entire length of the Colorado River through the Grand Canyon.)

The vans took us from Flagstaff to Lees Ferry, with a pit stop at the Cameron Trading Post. Eric was making sure we were off to a positive start by giving us a bathroom break after only being in the van for an hour. He must have figured at our age we needed it, and he was right.

The trading post was established over 100 years ago and has a motel, restaurant, RV park, and a gift shop, which sells every form of souvenir possible. Karen and I had been there many times before. We enjoy looking at their authentic Indian rugs. There are few places, if any that we've been to, that have higher quality rugs than the Cameron Trading Post. Often, a weaver will be there working on a rug.

Phill and I stood in front of a display of horseshoe-and-ring puzzles. Two horseshoes had been connected with chains forming a continuous loop. A metal ring is inside the loop. At first glance, it appears there is no way to free the metal ring from the loop. But there *is* a way, that's why it's a puzzle. I took one off the display rack and held it out toward Phill. "I bet you can't solve this by the time the vans are ready to leave," I said.

Phill reached for the puzzle, but it slipped out of his hand and landed on the floor. When it hit the floor, the metal ring freed itself and rolled across the store. "That doesn't count," I said. I grabbed another one and handed it to him. Phill unstuck the metal ring in less than five seconds and handed it back to me. "You have to put the ring back in the loop for it to count," I said. I was hoping that might confound him and I would save at least some face. He fiddled with the thing for a few minutes and the metal ring was back, trapped inside the loop.

"I like this game, Matt. What did we bet?" Phill asked.

I didn't answer him. I spent the next ten minutes trying to figure out the puzzle. A store employee had been listening to our exchange. Every couple of minutes she would walk past me and laugh. "Alright, you do it," I said to her finally. She just laughed and walked away.

The ride from Cameron to Lees Ferry took another hour and fifteen minutes. Lees Ferry is named after John D. Lee, who came to the area in 1870 to set up a ferry service to carry passengers and cargo across the Colorado River. In 1873 he established the ferry but was executed in 1877 for his role in the Mountain Meadows Massacre, which took place in Utah twenty years earlier.

Lee came to the area just a year after John Wesley Powell first navigated the Colorado River through the Grand Canyon. Northern Arizona at that time was a desolate place; most of the traffic was Mormon settlers and local Indians. The story is that Lee came to this area to escape the pursuit of law enforcement officers. While that may be true, it seems odd that someone who was trying to avoid capture would set up a business serving the public and put his name on it. Lee must not have believed the authorities would pursue him outside of Utah. In the end, he was gravely mistaken.

In the late nineteenth and early twentieth centuries, Lees Ferry was the only spot along the Colorado River where a ferry crossing was feasible. A ferry operated there from 1873 until 1929, when the first of the two Navajo Bridges was built a few miles downstream. Once the first Navajo bridge was open to traffic, there was no longer a need for the ferry service.

Lees Ferry is considered the beginning of the Grand Canyon, although the exact beginning and end can be hard to determine by just looking at a map. Today, most agree that the Grand Canyon is about 277 miles long as measured from the center of the Colorado River. Mile 0.0 is the gaging station at Lees Ferry. I say "about 277 miles" because at the western end of the canyon the waters from Lake Mead cause the Colorado River to widen past its natural banks. There's no spot along the river where one could say definitively that the river ends and the lake begins; the widening of the river is gradual. Just past mile 277 is the border between Grand Canyon National Park and Lake Mead National Recreational Area. That's generally accepted as the end of the canyon.

The edges, or rims, of the canyon are not in dispute. There is a distinct edge of the canyon on both sides of the river; "edge" is defined by where the surrounding plateau sharply drops in elevation toward the river. At its widest point, those edges are eighteen miles apart. And there are places where the canyon is over 6,000 feet deep. That's a big hole.

I couldn't find a cloud in the blue sky when we parked at the boat launch. The three support rafts and the other two dories were already in the water and tethered to the shore. The clear, green water made a stunning backdrop for the bright yellow rafts. When we got out of the van, we could feel that it was considerably warmer than when we left Flagstaff. I went to the restroom and peeled off the outer layer of clothes I had on. I also used the last flush toilet I would see for the next six days.

We had planned and prepared for two years, and now we were standing on the shore at Lees Ferry. While the drivers and boatmen put the two dories we'd towed from Flagstaff into the river, the passengers met the rest of the crew who had arrived earlier in the day. In total there were ten crewmembers: four dory boatmen (Eric, Andy, Rondo, and Andre), four raft boatmen (John "JB," Richard "Q," Maia [boatwoman], and Andrew), and two assistants (Betsy, and Brianne "B"). JB and Q took turns rowing one of the supply rafts. Along with the sixteen passengers, our group numbered twenty-six, the largest group the National Park Service allows on the river.

Each of the dories held four passengers and one boatman. They also carried cargo along with the boatman's gear. The bulk of the cargo and supplies were stored in the three inflatable rafts. I was amazed at the volume of stuff that fit in the seven boats. Not only did they carry all of the food— including ice to keep the perishables cold—for our six-day trip, they also carried all of the supplies for the second half of the trip as well, which was an additional eleven days. I had thought they would re-supply and off-load trash at Phantom Ranch, the mid-point of the trip, but they didn't. We learned that isn't practical.

Food was only a small portion of the cargo. There were also our sixteen large dry bags for our clothes and personal gear; sixteen additional large dry bags for our sleeping kits, sixteen full-sized sleep pads, the kitchen tables, gear and stove, more beer and wine than we needed for a week, latrine equipment, a couple of large boot bags, at least eight tents, twenty-six canvas folding chairs, a regulation-sized set of horse shoes (those are heavy) and, oh yeah, all of the personal gear for the ten crew members. We were hauling a lot of stuff, and the rafts didn't seem all that large to me.

It took about an hour to get the towed dories into the water, and all of the gear moved from the vans and loaded onto the rafts. While that was happening, Eric gave us instructions for sizing our life jackets and helmets. Once fitted, we each kept the same set for the entire week. From that moment forward we were responsible for keeping track of our life jacket and safety helmet, which amounted to making sure we secured them to something that wouldn't float away when we weren't using them.

Once the boats were ready to sail, Eric explained that he doesn't assign passengers to specific boats. It was our responsibility each day to find another couple to ride with and ask one of the dory boatmen if we could ride in his boat. Karen and I paired with John and Lolly on that first day. I went over to Andy and asked if the four of us could join him in his dory.

Besides being a dory boatman, Andy is a musician and a master dory boat builder. From the stories he shared with us, it sounded like much of his work involved fixing or restoring dories at his home in Colorado. On this trip, he was piloting a dory he owned named *Cottonwood*. It was a beautiful boat. It must have been about thirty years old but looked to be in near-perfect condition. Andy told us it was an excellent example of the "old checked plywood" style of dory.

It's common that the boatmen own the dory they guide on the river. On our trip, three of the four boatmen were using their own boat. In addition to Andre and Andy, Rondo, the fourth boatman, had brought his dory, the *Shoshone*. Each of the four dories varied slightly in design, but in general, they were very similar. During the week, we had the chance to ride in all four boats for at least one full day.

The *Cottonwood* had a flattened stern, which is typical of Grand Canyon dories. The truncated stern creates a flat section at the back of the boat that's perfect for a decorative design. A cottonwood leaf was painted there on Andy's boat. What I loved the most about the *Cottonwood* was its colors.

Andy used the same colors that Martin Litton had back in the early days: white, red and green. But not just any white, red and green.

The story goes that Litton started guiding on the river with a gentleman by the name of P.T. Reilly in the late 1950s. Reilly wanted a color scheme for his boats that would fit in well with the magnificent setting of the Grand Canyon. Reilly asked a neighbor, Harper Goff, who was an art director at Disney for his help. Goff suggested the three-color scheme of Refrigerator White, Cadillac Aztec Red and Willy's Beryl Green. Reilly went with Goff's suggestion. Later, when Reilly exited the business, and Litton filled the void by creating Grand Canyon Dories, he adopted the same color scheme for his boats. Today, however, O.A.R.S. doesn't follow the Goff color scheme.

When we were ready to board the boats, Rondo called for our attention and said, "We have a tradition that brings us good luck on the river. The tradition is this: whenever we shove off, I say 'dories,' and all of you say 'ho.' Got it?" We all nodded in agreement and said, "Got it." Our river trip was starting to take on the feel of a summer camp adventure.

The crew on the support rafts had climbed aboard and were patiently waiting for the rest of us to awkwardly climb into our dories. The dories were beached stern-first, so to get to our seats at the front of the boat, John and I had to walk across the deck. I was hesitant about stepping on the clean deck of Andy's boat in my sandy, wet sandals. During the week, we would get better at climbing in and out of the dories without covering the deck with mud or sand. But making a mess was inevitable; that's what the sponges were for that were tucked into the handholds next to the passenger benches: to swab the deck.

When all of the boats were ready to shove off, Rondo yelled, "Dories!" We enthusiastically shouted, "Ho!" We were off. A few yards away from shore John turned to me and said, "Who is Doris?"

There was a gentle breeze. The sun was shining. It was a

brilliant day. Despite the rain earlier in the week, the Colorado River was clear and gave off an emerald green reflection.

A mile from where we'd launched, I noticed that the west side of the riverbank looked like it had a flat, muddy shoreline. The mud must have been due to the recent rains. As we continued further I could see that the shoreline wasn't just muddy, it was moving. In fact, it wasn't a shoreline at all. It was the Paria River merging into the Colorado River. The water coming in was thick and brown. Plant debris, sticks, and small logs floated in the muddy water. For another hundred yards or so our dory glided through the clear water while we watched the mud flow get closer. Eventually, the waters merged, and we were floating in a river of cocoa. John looked toward the back of the boat where Karen was sitting and yelled, "What time will you be bathing in the river this afternoon? I can't wait to watch."

Over the course of the next week, the river cleared a bit, but it would still be more cloudy than clear when we reached Phantom Ranch, eighty-nine miles downriver.

The walls of the canyon rose quickly as soon as we passed the mouth of the Paria. At the three and a half mile point on the river, we came to the Navajo Bridges, where the sides of the canyon are nearly 500 feet tall.

There are two Navajo Bridges that run parallel to each other about a hundred feet apart. They look almost identical, but the oldest was completed in 1929, the newer in 1997. They are both 467 feet above the river. The older bridge was built to carry automobile traffic and was adequate in its day. By the end of the twentieth century though, it no longer met the state's bridge standards and was deemed obsolete. Now, the newer bridge is open to motor vehicles and is part of Highway 89. The 1929 bridge remains open for horse and foot traffic only.

Pedestrians were standing on the footbridge above us as we floated beneath it. They may have been waving, but it was hard to tell, they were barely visible. As we looked up, we could also see several California condors circling in the sky. The condors seemed to follow us for the next half of a mile or so. For me, the bridges were a gateway into the wilderness. We wouldn't see another bridge for eighty-five miles.

It didn't take long for us to feel as if we were the only ones on the river. There had been a group of rafters at Lees Ferry preparing to launch at the same time we were there. I thought maybe we would see them often during the week because their start time was so close to ours, but it would be a couple of days before we saw them again. About once a day we would briefly intersect another float trip. These meetings rarely lasted more than ten to twenty minutes. A few times we saw hikers on the cliffs above the river, and once a group of hikers who made it all the way to the river. These encounters were always brief, and for most of the trip, we felt we were alone in the wilderness.

Rapid-wise, the river was relatively calm on the first day. We encountered riffles at mile 3 and mile 6. It wasn't until mile 8 that we went through an area classified as a rapid. There, at Jackass Canyon, we floated through Badger Creek Rapid. At Badger, the river drops about fifteen feet causing a rapid rated 4-6 in difficulty. (And no, they didn't name Jackass Canyon after John. It's merely a coincidence.)

The rapids in the Grand Canyon are not rated using the International Scale of River Difficulty, which ranges from I to VI (usually designated with Roman Numerals). Instead, they use a scale from 1 to 10, with ten being the most difficult. There is no universally agreed upon conversion for translating a rating from one system to the other. It's not clear to me why people use an alternative scale for the big water rivers in the western U.S., but it's good to know which system is being used when you're reading a description of a rapid. When I tell people who are familiar with the international scale (which is much more commonly used) that we ran a 4-6 rapid on our first day in the Grand Canyon, they're shocked. The American Whitewater organization, which maintains the international scale, describes a class VI rapid as *"runs [that] have almost never been attempted and often exemplify the extremes of difficulty, unpredictability, and danger. The consequences of errors are very severe, and rescue may be impossible."* There are no rapids in the Grand Canyon this severe.

Downstream from Lees Ferry, Mother Nature laid out the river as if to gradually introduce us to white water. After the first couple of riffles, there were a few medium-sized rapids before the end of the first day. The boatmen described the Colorado River to us as a "pool drop" river, as opposed to a "continuous rapid" river. Pool drop means that there are stretches of calm, slow-moving water, which is flat like a pool or lake. Then, the river drops and flows over obstructions that cause rapids. Debris, mostly in the form of large rocks and boulders, carried by flash floods from side canyons is the most common cause of rapids in the Grand Canyon.

At mile 11, we ran what would be the roughest rapid of the day, Soap Creek Rapid. There the river dropped sixteen feet forming a 5-6 rapid. It was an exhilarating run. I'm sure it required a lot of skill on the part of the boatmen to keep us right-side up through the rough water. That's probably why I never felt that what we were doing was dangerous. That said, I could now see how a wrong move by the boatman or a rogue wave could easily cause one of our little boats to flip.

Past Soap Creek Rapid the sidewalls of the canyon were steep. In the afternoon there's not much direct sun on the river. The temperature was dropping, and it was time to find a place to camp for the night. According to the Belknap's Waterproof Grand Canyon River Guide that O.A.R.S. sent us, there are 257 campsites listed by the National Park Service along the 277 miles of the Colorado River in the park. Eric, as the lead boatman, was always at the front of our flotilla. He was slowly rowing and appeared to be examining every rock and feature of the canyon as we moved downstream. One thing that struck me was the intensity of the boatmen's interest in the canyon. These guys had all guided dory trips through the canyon countless times, yet they were like kids seeing it for the first time. Their passion was contagious.

Eric piloting the *Marble Canyon* on the Colorado River.
Navajo Bridges in the distance.

ARRIVING AT CAMP

Sixteen miles from our starting point at Lees Ferry, the dories began slowly edging toward the shore. Eric had chosen the campsite about a mile upstream of House Rock Rapid called Hot Na Na. Karen asked Andy if Hot Na Na meant "attractive grandmother" in English. He gave her a confused look, and then said, "Hey, I'm going to need one of you guys in the front to step out a few feet from shore and pull us in."

John jumped out and held onto the bow of the boat. He pulled it onto the beach so the rest of us could climb out. We had to be careful where we stepped, the mud from the Paria was settling on the beach in thick pockets. Karen stepped over the side of the dory and sank mid-shin into the chocolate-colored mud. With the rest of us safely on shore, Karen declined our offers of help, so we watched while she struggled mightily. First, she lifted one leg out of the water, which put all of her weight on the other leg causing it to sink deeper into the mud. Then she placed the free leg back onto the muddy river bottom and pulled the other leg up while the previously liberated leg disappeared into the muck. Karen repeated this several times. On one try, her foot came out of the water with no shoe attached. Despite expending huge effort, she didn't seem to be getting closer to dry sand, which was about two arm lengths away. I wondered how long it would take before she lost her balance completely and went under, but she managed to stay mostly above water.

Eventually, she got to a spot in the river that had a firm, sandy bottom and was able to begin washing the mud off her legs. I extended my hand and said, "Let me help you out of there, Hot Na Na."

She splashed her way out, grabbed my extended hand and tried to pull me into the river. I retired the Hot Na Na nickname after that.

The beach where we landed was our home for the evening. Each campsite is rated small, medium or large based on the usable space. With twenty-six people in our group, we were limited to using the larger campsites on the river. Each couple only required a small patch of sand to set up their sleeping area, but the campsite also needed to be big enough to accommodate the food preparation area and the chair circle. Our dories and supply rafts carried enough chairs for everyone in the group to have a place to sit. The chair circle is where we ate meals and visited at night. One of the crew told me, "The camp chairs are a fairly new addition. Years ago we didn't bring chairs, so everyone had to sit on the sand to eat. That cut down on the nightly conversation. People got tired of sitting on the ground and would go to bed earlier."

The food preparation area consisted of a gas grill, several tables—a couple of which had stainless steel tops—and a variety of coolers and containers that held all of the cooking implements and food for our meals.

It was never clear what the crew's expectation was for how involved we should be in the numerous tasks required to live on the river for a week: unloading and loading the boats, setting up tents, making the chair circle, unpacking and assembling the mess tables and equipment, etc. People we'd spoken to who had been on guided river trips told us they never "lifted a finger." But on this trip, we were eager to pitch in and help. However, more than once while we were "helping" I could read the look on the crew's face as if to say, "Stop it and go have a beer." Still, we knew if we all shared the heavy lifting, it would get done much quicker, and we could all move on to other vital tasks like trying to find the perfect place to sleep for the night.

Being on the river for a week with our group reminded me of one of those corporate management offsite events where the participants are given vague, difficult tasks, so they learn how to solve problems together and find out who the true leaders are. We got along well with each other, very well, but let me just say, our group of passengers will not be forming a company to solve the important problems of the world anytime soon.

We started unloading the boats with what seemed to be a solid plan. We would form a line starting at one of the supply rafts and run it to the spot on shore where all of the stuff needed to land, passing the cargo from person to person like an old-fashioned bucket brigade. Then we would move the line to the next boat and repeat until we'd unloaded all of the boats. That was the plan. It went well until the crew began handing us the dry bags, which contained our clothing and personal stuff. As soon as one person in line recognized their bag, they would take it and walk away, leaving a gap in the line. This seemingly small disruption was more than the group could recover from. Soon we dissolved into a mob surrounding the back of the boat, each of us with our hands held out as if we were shoppers at Wal-Mart the day after Thanksgiving begging for the last deeply-discounted big-screen TV.

All of the cargo managed to eventually make it ashore that first night. Each successive night we invented new and even more inefficient ways to unload the boats. One night we mostly sat on the beach and watched while Bart and Mark unloaded all of the boats by themselves. That may have been our fastest unloading of the trip.

At first, the area where we'd landed didn't seem large enough to accommodate all of our tents plus space for the kitchen and chair circle. We realized, however, once we started poking around that there were plenty of flat patches of sand where we could set up a tent.

With the boats unloaded we each found the dry bag and sleep kit that belonged to us. My instinct was to quickly scout out the perfect place to call home for the evening. I learned that first night though, not to be too quick to choose our spot. Instead, one must wait to see where the crew establishes the latrine area, and then make sure to be a safe distance away. Not because of the smell, but to avoid the constant traffic.

Karen and I claimed a spot close to Phill and Wendy and two other couples about fifty yards from the kitchen area. O.A.R.S. provided every couple with a tent, but several couples scoffed at the thought of sleeping in one and opted instead to sleep under the stars. I was inspired by their enthusiasm for the open air and suggested to Karen that we do the same. She scrunched her face and said, "I'm not sleeping out in the open where things can crawl across my body." She convinced me with her mention of things crawling across her/my body. Tent it would be.

Being our first night on the river, Rondo came to our area and offered to show us all how to set up a tent. I politely laughed and said under my breath, "Show us how to set up a tent? *Please.*" Phill, who had plenty of experience with sleeping outdoors and setting up tents, was delighted to act like he was clueless so Rondo would use Phill's tent as the demo.

I busied myself with laying down our tarp as I ignored the tent seminar, which lasted five minutes and ended with a completely assembled, taut tent ready for occupancy. Another five minutes later Phill and Wendy had their temporary home organized and were heading back to the supply boats for a beer.

Forty-five minutes later—after I had bandaged the cut on my finger where I nicked it on one of the tent poles—I shoved the "extra" pieces of our tent in the corner of the vestibule and began laying out our sleep mats and sleeping bags inside. All was well until I tried to zip close the door flap.

"Something is not right with this tent," I said to Karen.

"Maybe you should have used all of the pieces," she replied while pointing to the pile of leftovers. In my defense, the only extra pieces were a few tent stakes and a pole splice, which we didn't need.

I wouldn't have it. "The flap to our tent's door is too small for the opening. It won't zip closed. This must be a defective tent. That's the only possible explanation because any idiot can set up a tent…"

"How about we move this corner of the tent over a few inches like this?" Karen asked.

Miraculously our tent healed itself and I was able to zip the door flap closed effortlessly.

"Show us how to set up a tent? Please!" I said to myself.

By now there was a nip in the air, and I was concerned about how much beer time I had lost due to the defective tent. I opened my dry bag to get a pair of long johns to put on under my shorts, but it took me a while to put my hands on them. I had to open every freezer bag to find my long johns. I put them on and headed toward the chair circle to join the rest of the group.

In the months leading up to the trip, there were several conversation threads among the male passengers about beer. The most important question was, "How do they keep the beer cold?" Surely they couldn't keep all of our beer – and the next group's – on ice for the entire trip. This was in the back of our minds while we were standing around waiting to shove off from Lees Ferry. One of the guys in our group finally asked, "How do you keep the beer cold?" JB responded quickly with a well-rehearsed answer, "Don't worry gentlemen, the beer is perfectly chilled at all times. We place the cans at the bottom of my raft, and they sit in the frigid river water. At the end of the day, the beer is a chilly 50 degrees."

We all looked at each other and whispered, "Fifty degrees? Did he say 50 degrees? What temperature is beer normally?" We were concerned, but weren't sure we needed to be.

Storing the beer at the bottom of JB's raft was also an ingenious idea for another reason: it forced us to completely unload the rafts each night to get to the beer. It's also why the crew always insisted that we unload JB's raft last.

At the bottom of the beer raft, the cans were several layers deep. The trick was to dig to the bottom to get the coolest one. I asked JB, "How do we know whose beer we're drinking?"

"Look at the bottom of the can."

On the bottom of each can were the initials of the passenger who ordered that beer. "OK, got it," I replied.

I was looking for a couple of cans with "MS" on the bottom for Karen and I. The first can I pulled out was a CW; that was Craig's beer. The next was an MH, then a PR. This task was becoming harder than I thought it would be. The next nine or ten beers had PR written on their bottoms; those were Phill's. No matter where I fished in the mass of cans I pulled out PR's.

I hollered at Phill, "How much beer did you order?"

"Matt, have a beer on me, and relax."

I never found an MS that first night, but it was clear that as a group we weren't going to run out in the next six days, so Karen and I drank on Phill's tab.

Karen setting up at our sleeping area. This photo was from our third night on the river.

Hot Na Na Camp

THE BAKERY

Originally, I had not intended to write in detail about the latrine. But from our conversations with people who are contemplating going on a river trip, we've learned that this is a topic in which many are interested. It's not so much that they want to know the details. Rather, the lack of information about it causes them considerable anxiety. I hope this description will help people who are considering a river trip put this anxiety behind them. Here we go. (Shameless puns intended.)

Being that it was our first night out, the crew needed to explain some of the nuances of living on the river. Andy was the lucky boatman who got the chore of giving us the hygiene orientation.

Staying healthy was vital to us having a happy and harmonious week together. Given the communal nature of the kitchen, food preparation, and eating areas, hand washing was mandatory. You must wash your hands after you visit the latrine, and before you approach the meal table. Andy was polite as he delivered the cleanliness speech, but he was serious, as he should have been. "If we see you not wash your hands, we'll call you out on it. We have to," he said. Any illness in camp would spread immediately if the group didn't adhere to a strict cleanliness routine. We were fortunate that everyone in our group remained healthy throughout the trip. That's not always how it goes.

The crew had stories about trips where one person catches a virus, and the entire group gets sick. There have even been times when a virus from one sick group sickened the next group who camped at the same site on a subsequent night. Given that there is no easy way to get a sick person out of the canyon, everyone on the river needs to do what they can to minimize the preventable spread of germs.

Next was the bathroom talk. Other than the fear of flipping over and drowning in a rapid, going to the bathroom in the wilderness creates the most anxiety amongst first-time river-goers. I can't speak for anyone else, but this was the source of worry for me before the trip. Now that the trip is over, I can say that my anxiety was unnecessary. Still, living for a week in the wilderness is not the same as staying at a Hampton Inn.

To start, a river trip in the Grand Canyon is strictly a "pack it in, pack it out" trip. Meaning, everything we brought with us had to be packed out, with very few exceptions. We could pee, bathe and brush our teeth in the river, but that was about it. (Regarding what type of soap we could use in the river, O.A.R.S. trip planning literature stated, "*We recommend using a liquid biodegradable soap such as Campsuds or Dr. Bronner's.*)

The rule for peeing was you had to go in the river or a bucket. The buckets were then emptied into the river. As Eric told us, "Dilution is the solution to pollution on the river." There was a time in the past when it was acceptable for river rafters to pee on the ground away from the river, but eventually that turned the campsites into giant, smelly litter boxes due to the small amount of rainfall in the canyon.

With twenty-six people doing number one in the river we needed some basic pee traffic control. Andy told us that when we stop during the day for lunch or hikes, and there is no latrine set up, the rule of the river is "skirts up, pants down." This apt phrase meant that women were supposed to head upstream from the boats to find a place to go and men downstream. Following this simple rule would give the women at least a fighting chance at privacy. I must not have been paying attention when Andy told us this rule. For the next couple of days, every time I started walking upriver with determination one of the women passengers would yell, "Skirts up, pants down!" I thought, "What does that mean and why are you yelling it at me?" Finally, Karen pulled me aside and explained.

"That's why the women all go together because you guys keep wandering upstream," she said.

Apparently, I wasn't the only guy who didn't understand the rule. The women would head upstream, try to find large boulders near the edge of the water to hide behind, and then form a half-circle facing outward, surrounding the woman whose turn it was to pee. When a guy would approach, the women standing guard would yell, "Skirts up, pants down! Geeeez!"

The river has a slight tide, a daily rise and fall in level, due to Glen Canyon Dam releasing water at different rates during the day. There were times when the tide was out and left a band of wet sand at the shoreline. The wet area made it difficult to pee so that you "hit" the river without having to step (or squat) in the mud. In those instances, hitting wet sand or mud was acceptable.

Depending on the time of day, the woman weren't always required to pee in the river. If our camp was set up and they didn't like the idea of "hitting the river," there was a pee bucket in the latrine area. The crew also provided us with small blue buckets we could take to our campsites in the evening to pee in rather than trying to make our way to and from the river or latrine in the middle of the night.

On our first night out, I thought this was a ridiculous idea and decided it would be much easier to stand at the edge of the river and do my business. So, at 2:00 am, half asleep, in a strange place, without wearing my contacts I stood on the uneven sand and nearly went face-first into the water. My middle-of-the-night close call taught me to be sure I knew where my little blue bucket was before falling asleep.

Peeing though, wasn't the greatest source of concern amongst the passengers. After the pee talk, Andy explained the rest of the latrine set up. Each day when we landed at our campsite for the evening, the crew would find a secluded, out-of-the-way area to place the potty. The system was well thought out. At a safe distance from the toilet, there was a hand washing station, which consisted of hand soap, a bucket of filtered river water, a spigot connected to a foot pump and a drain bucket. Everyone coming out of the latrine must wash his or her hands. The crew also placed roadside reflectors along the trail leading from the hand washing station to the latrine. The reflectors were a lifesaver when it was dark out.

The toilet was a small box about two feet by two feet wide and the height of your toilet at home. (If you don't have a toilet at home, I'm sorry.) It had a lid that could be sealed shut to keep the contents contained when the crew carried it to and from the raft. Campers and river goers have nicknamed these boxes "groovers." Why groover? There was a time when they didn't have butt-friendly seats. The box just had a hole at the top, and the edge of the box would leave a groove on the user's bottom. Finally, after years of grooved backsides, some genius came up with the idea of attaching a traditional toilet seat to the box and—no more grooves, but the name stuck.

Andy explained that our groover was a chemical toilet, meaning that chemicals are applied to the waste to reduce odor and speed the composting process. Next to the groover was a plastic container of white powder that you sprinkled onto the contents of the toilet after you're finished. Andy explained, "You just sprinkle this white stuff on, you know, what you left in the box. Kind of like sprinkling powdered sugar on a donut." Nice. I could have lived without that imagery. That's how the latrine got the nickname "The Bakery."

The groover was for number two. There was a pee bucket next to it for number one. It was acceptable to put toilet paper from your groover-business into the groover. It was not acceptable to put toilet paper from your pee-business in the pee bucket. That had to be placed into a separate plastic bag so it could be packed out. The reason for this, of course, was that the pee bucket got dumped into the river when we broke down camp and you can't dump toilet paper in the river.

We only had one "toilet paper in the pee bucket" violation on the entire trip. Lolly. She forgot and violated the rule. Her blunder caused her considerable guilt. It ate at her. All morning she fidgeted nervously. She couldn't eat. She couldn't make eye contact. None of us knew her secret. We became worried about her. Then she came out with it, "Eric, I'm sorry, I put toilet paper in the pee bucket!" she announced.

"I know. I fished it out. You get to fish out the next one," Eric replied.

Now, you might ask, as I did before the orientation was over, "How will one know if someone is occupying the latrine? Are we supposed to whistle while we're in there?" This sent a shot of fear through Karen. She can't whistle. Thankfully that was not the correct answer. The key was the toilet paper, literally. There would be only one roll of toilet paper in use at any time. When the person using the latrine returned to the hand washing station, they must place the roll next to the hand wash bucket. This would be the only signal that the latrine was unoccupied. If there was no roll of toilet paper sitting next to the hand wash bucket, do NOT go to the latrine.

The peaceful coexistence of the group depended on everyone respecting this rule, and also the hand-washing rule. There were only a couple of times when someone would fail to bring the key back with them, each time resulting in a line up at the hand washing station. As soon as there were twenty-six people in line we would realize that someone forgot to bring the key back with them from the latrine. Or, if ten minutes went by without the toilet paper returning, we would send a discovery party toward the toilet area. Fortunately, those expeditions never found anyone, just a lonely roll of toilet paper resting next to the groover.

The latrine arrangement was all well and good, but we would be spending half of our time away from camp, on the river or hiking. What then? Andy said they had an emergency kit if anyone needed to go number two when the latrine wasn't set up.

Karen later asked me, "How do you think that works? What if you are having an 'emergency' in the dory?"

I'm not sure how the emergency procedure would work on a dory. I guess we would row to shore. If we couldn't get to shore in time then–I don't know. No one asked, and the situation never presented itself.

Finally, Andy had special instructions just for the women. He reached down and grabbed an old army surplus ammo can that had "Fem. Kit" stenciled on the side. As soon as Andy said, "Now, for the women who might need to…" all of the husbands headed back toward the center of camp. As I was walking away, I looked back to see Andy and the wives in serious conversation. There was a lot of head nodding and looking in the ammo can. A few minutes later, standing in the middle of camp, we heard the women off in the distance explode into laughter. Andy appeared out of the bushes by himself shaking his head. We gave him one of our beers for being a good sport.

The Bakery

The hand wash station. Notice there is no key.

DINNER

Watching the crew set up the camp kitchen was like watching a magic trick where the magician endlessly pulls things out of his hat. Every evening, from out of the bottom of the rafts came all the equipment and supplies needed to cook dinner and breakfast for twenty-six people. Yeti coolers kept the perishable foods cold for the entire trip. And those huge coolers all fit into the bottom of the rafts as well. It's surprising that those rafts still rode above the waterline once loaded.

Each night our meals were prepared by one of the dory boatmen and one or two of the other crewmembers. The boatmen and crew rotated their kitchen duties each meal. To keep us occupied and out of their way, they would put out munchies while they prepared the evening meal. Our pre-dinner ritual was to stand around, eat snacks, have a drink and talk about the day's events. That first night we were still getting to know the boatmen and crew.

Andre, besides being a geologist, is a lifelong dory boatman. Martin Litton talked him into rowing dories for Grand Canyon Dories in the early 1970s, and he has been rowing dories ever since. Rondo is also a lifer, and also had the good fortune to guide dory trips through the Grand Canyon with Martin Litton. When he isn't on the water, you can find him in the cycle and paddle board shop he owns in Colorado.

John Blaustein, who was in charge of one of the support rafts, goes by "JB." He had been one of the first boatmen Martin Litton hired when he started Grand Canyon Dories in the 1960s. On his first trip with Litton, JB was a cook's assistant, but he got the chance to row a few stretches of the river to see what it was like. Litton promoted JB to boatman on his second trip and put him in charge of a passenger dory. That was fifty years ago. Like the dory boatmen, JB looked years younger than his age.

During his decades on the river, JB became an accomplished photographer. He had brought with him a copy of the latest edition of his book *The Hidden Canyon: A River Journey*. We all took turns looking at the beautiful photos in his book. For the remainder of the trip, passengers were constantly asking him questions about the river and his experiences. "You have to tell us some of your secrets, JB. How did you get these amazing shots?" someone asked.

"You have to remember that I've been doing this for a very long time. But as a photographer friend once told me, 'The two most important things to remember about taking great photos are: F8 and be there.' I've been very fortunate to 'be there' to get some fantastic photos."

Another crewmember was Richard Quartaroli. The only reason I know his name is because someone had brought on the trip a copy of the spring 2016 edition of the *boatman's quarterly review*, which featured him. No one called him Richard on our trip; he went simply by "Q."

Q became a professional Grand Canyon river guide in 1975. He is also a historian. He knows just about everything one could know regarding the history of the Colorado River and, in particular, about John Wesley Powell. Our crew had a wealth of knowledge, and we got to hang out and learn from them all week.

Maia was the captain of one of the supply rafts. She had recently graduated from Columbia University, but as she said to me on one of our afternoon hikes, "I knew I wanted to be a boatman before I ever went off to college." Her father was a boatman, and she grew up learning the business. Maia was now getting her chance to do it full time. She seemed to love every minute of it, except maybe those first couple of moments each morning when she sat up in her boat and asked herself, "Where the hell am I?"

Another member of the crew was Andrew from Bend, Oregon. Andrew was in his late 20s and had the honor of being the captain of the poo-boat. Kevin Fedarko would call him the "groover boy," the person in charge of setting up, taking down, and transporting the latrine. Andrew is in good company. Kevin Fedarko wrote a blog post about his experience also being a groover boy, at the age of forty-three. But don't feel sorry for Kevin—or Andrew—Kevin went on to write *The Emerald Mile*, which I referenced earlier.

Rounding out the crew were Brianne and Betsy. Like Q, Brianne went by "B." I didn't even know her full first name until the last day on the river. B was a friend of Rondo's, who had invited her on the trip. B has two little ones at home, and when she asked her husband what he thought about her spending a couple of weeks on the river he said, "Go for it!" This was her first time through the canyon as a crewmember.

It wasn't Betsy's first trip through the canyon. She'd been doing it for years, sometimes as a passenger and sometimes as a crewmember. Like all of the crew, Betsy was a delight to be around: energetic, always smiling, and funny. She now makes her home in New Mexico, but you don't have to talk to Betsy for more than a minute to hear her Texas drawl. She taught us one of the most crucial tips about river travel. For passengers who ordered box wine for the trip, O.A.R.S. took the inner bag of wine out of the box it came in and put them each in a canvas bag that had a hook on top. Like the beer cans, someone had labeled each bag with the initials of the person who had ordered the wine. Each night the crew would hang all of the wine bags on the serving tables by the kitchen area. Betsy had the brilliant idea of hanging her bag on the back of her chair in the chair circle so she wouldn't have to walk back to the mess area to refill her cup. This, and her Texas drawl, made her instant friends with all of the women passengers.

One of the most common responses we got when we told people we were going on a river trip was, "I hear the meals are incredible. They serve gourmet meals on those trips." There seems to be a widely-held belief that all river trips through the Grand Canyon serve gourmet meals. That's not the case. The food on our trip was fantastic, but it wasn't gourmet. If you're planning a river trip and you expect gourmet meals, make sure the trip description says so.

A boatman told me that he doesn't like guiding on gourmet trips because they can't spend as much time on the river. The meals take so long to prepare that they have to stay on shore for longer than non-gourmet trips. Usually on gourmet trips, one of the crew is the dedicated chef, and the other crewmembers spend extra time helping prepare meals.

I hadn't paid much attention to the description of the meals before we signed up for the trip, but I was glad we chose the trip we did. The food was great; I was never hungry or felt I didn't get enough to eat. In fact, I was surprised the first night when I saw the camp grill covered with enough salmon fillets to feed the entire group plus have enough leftover to eat with our eggs the next morning.

Each day we ate breakfast and dinner in the chair circle. At every campsite, the crew would find a spot big enough to place the twenty-six camp chairs in a big circle. Plates on laps and drinks in the sand, that was the routine. The drinking containers O.A.R.S. gave us at the start of the trip were an upgrade from the old Sierra Club cups that passengers were issued in the early days when Martin Litton was running trips. Ours were stainless steel insulated Klean Kanteens that held twelve ounces and had a plastic screw off safety lid. JB told me that in the early days all meals and drinks were served in the Sierra Club cups. He said, "You could have coffee and oatmeal for breakfast, just not at the same time."

It was interesting hearing the crew talk about "back in the day." They made it sound like the trips of old were roughing it compared to now: they didn't have chairs to sit on or lights except for headlamps, there were no plates, and no groovers if you can imagine that.

Another aspect of river life that's changed since the early days is the number of ants in camp. Red ants are still common at the sandy campsites along the river, but the boatmen told us that there are fewer of them now than in the past. The ants in the Grand Canyon are Red Harvester Ants, not to be confused with Fire Ants. We saw red ants on our trip, but I never felt they were a nuisance. They typically don't sting unless they are aggravated (like being stepped on), or if they sense you are threatening their nest.

There are fewer ants in the canyon these days because of the efforts of the guide companies and river travelers to reduce micro trash (crumbs of food). Red Harvester Ants thrive on crumbs. Take away the crumbs, and there are fewer ants. It's as simple as that. The crew placed mats underneath the food preparation tables at each campsite. The mats caught most of the stray food bits, and we were encouraged to not let any food drop on the ground when we ate our meals or snacks. Same for when we washed our dishes or threw away food wrappers. Every morsel of food we could keep off the ground was one less meal for the ants. As one of the boatmen said, "Ants eat the crumbs, and when they have plenty to eat they make more ants."

With thousands of people a year traveling through the Grand Canyon along the Colorado River, every trace of food left behind by humans adds up quickly.

The crew was meticulous about the dish-washing. Cleaning up after dinner for twenty-six people goes quickly if everyone pitches in. The dishwashing routine involved four large, metal pots. Most of the dinner plates looked as if they were licked clean before we started washing them, but we scraped anything left on them into a trash bag. Then the plates went into the first pot, the pre-wash. Each washing container had a scrubber so we could get our dishes progressively cleaner as we moved down the line. One of the crew would heat water on the stove and fill the last tub with scalding hot, clear water; that's where we gave our dishes and utensils a final rinse. We each placed our clean plates in a mesh pocket that hung off the washing table and our forks in a clean silverware container. The crew strained the dishwater before dumping it back into the river. The captured food chunks got packed out.

JB was on kitchen clean up duty the first night. He was swirling his hand around the bottom of the pre-wash pot, "Where is all of this sand coming from? Hey, everybody, brush off the bottom of your plates before washing them. We don't want to pack out half the beach." The amount of sand that made it into the washing buckets each night was directly correlated to how much beer we drank that evening. Whenever one of the passengers would approach the washing station, they would hear, "Sand," reminding them to brush off the bottom of their plate.

Andy, B, and Maia fixing dinner.

HOT NA NA CAMP

With our plate-washing duty finished, it was time for the crew to make a campfire. Another technique they used to protect the campsite was to put down a fire mat before making a campfire. Once everyone was finished eating dinner, the crew would place the mat in the center of the chair circle and then place the coal box from the grill on top of the mat. Inside the coal box, which was maybe a foot and a half wide by three feet long, the crew would burn firewood. They didn't make a fire every night because the only wood they could burn was what they had brought with them. The National Park Service does not allow collecting or burning driftwood found in the canyon from March through October. (The acceptable driftwood collection dates change from time to time.)

Having a fire after dinner was a real treat and a surprise. "They brought fire wood?" I wondered. That's yet another rabbit pulled out of the magician's raft. It was a classic scene, sixteen middle-aged people in long johns and sweatshirts, stuffed and satisfied, staring into a roaring campfire. It seemed like forever ago that we were all sitting under fluorescent lights at the DoubleTree Hotel introducing ourselves. We were now in a different world.

You don't want to be the first one in the group to call it a night and go to bed, especially on the first night of the trip. At least you don't announce it to the group and risk killing the campfire buzz. One at a time, people would go back to their tent as if they were just retrieving a jacket to stay warm, but then they wouldn't return. Karen had been gone for five minutes; I got the hint. It was bedtime.

Most of the crew had already packed it in for the night. I didn't know what time it was, but it seemed early. After they had put the kitchen in order for the next morning, they readied their sleeping areas and crashed. It surprised me how fast they went from bustling around camp to lying motionless in their sleeping bags.

Unless it was raining, the boatmen slept on their boats. Each of them slept on their deck on top of a sleeping pad with a footprint not much bigger than their bodies. One of the last steps of their end-of-day routine was to check their lines. Every time we made it to shore, each boatman would pound an anchor into the sand with a mallet, and then tie their boat to the anchor. If you are sleeping on a boat, you want to make absolutely certain that you've firmly buried the anchor and tied the line securely. I've heard stories of a boatman waking in the middle of the night to the roar of approaching rapids as he drifted downriver.

By the time I made it from the campfire to our sleeping area, Karen had already snuggled into her sleeping bag. We'd done a good job keeping sand out of our tent, which wasn't easy. Our shoes stayed outside in the vestibule under the rain fly. After the first night, we both got into the habit of pounding our shoes upside down on a rock before we put them back on. If any critters had made a home inside our shoes while we were sleeping, we wanted to make sure to give them a chance to vacate.

The tents that O.A.R.S. provided were wide enough to fit two of the yellow sleeping pads that came with our sleep kits; the crew called them Paco pads. They were a bit of a pain to carry a long way to our sleeping area, but it was well worth the inconvenience for the added comfort all night long. Next to our pads there was just enough room on the tent floor for us to put all the stuff we thought we might need in the middle of the night: glasses, flip flops, headlamp, contact case, and water.

The evening air was chilly, and it felt comfortable inside our tent after I zipped the door shut. That lasted about five minutes. I heard exaggerated exhales coming from Karen's sleeping bag each time I would sit up and adjust the vents. I was baking like a potato. Eventually, I had every screened opening unzipped, and I was lying on top—not inside—my sleeping bag. "Are you hot?" I asked Karen.

"I wasn't until you woke me up," she replied.

"We should have slept outside," I said.

"I'm too tired to move my stuff outside. We can sleep under the stars tomorrow night," she said.

During the evening, it became cooler inside the tent, but it was still muggy.

The first night's sleep in a new place is always fitful for me. Having not slept much the night before in Flagstaff though, I managed a few long stretches of uninterrupted slumber. I must have missed the part of the orientation when they told us they would blow a conch shell each morning when coffee was ready. Even so, when I heard it, I knew what it meant.

I managed to put my contacts into my eyes without sand on them. My O.A.R.S. steel mug was right next to my sleeping bag. I grabbed it and looked for Karen's; I was going to bring her coffee, but she was already getting out of her bag. We walked together to the chair circle.

"How did you sleep last night?" I asked her.

"Fair. It was stuffy in the tent. And you flipped around like a fish at the bottom of a boat," she replied.

"Yeah, we need to try sleeping outside tonight. It's warmer down here at the bottom of the canyon than I thought it would be."

The meal crew for that morning was busy preparing for breakfast. It then made sense why they had gone to bed so early. It was only 6:00 am, and it looked like they had been up for quite awhile. A large canteen of coffee was already sitting on one of the serving tables.

It would take me a couple of days to adjust to river time. By 6:15 am I had my coffee and was asking the crew what was for breakfast. I didn't get an answer, just a look that I understood meant, "Go away!" Karen said to me, "Leave them alone, they don't want to be bothered this early in the morning."

Karen was right; the crew didn't need me in their hair while they were fixing breakfast. Back at our sleeping area I broke down our tent and packed it in its nylon bag. I was very proud of myself for getting all of the parts into the bag; they barely fit. Except I had forgotten to pack the rainfly. Everything had to come out of the bag so I could refold it, this time with the rainfly included. Finally! I'd squeezed everything into the bag. Karen and I had all of our clothes and gear laid out on the blue tarp we'd placed under the tent the night before to serve as a ground cover. As she was organizing her stuff, she found the tent stakes and handed them to me, "Did you forget these, Mr. Camper?" Crap!

That morning at Hot Na Na we had to make sure we set aside our rain gear before we packed our large dry bags. Soon after shoving off, we would be running the first difficult rapid of the trip, House Rock Rapid, and we would need it. We both brought rain pants and jackets, as well as neoprene socks. O.A.R.S. suggests on their packing list that you bring water booties or wet socks to wear on your feet in the dory. It was a good thing we'd seen that piece of advice about a year before the trip because it took that long for us to each find a pair that fit.

I went back to packing after breakfast. My large dry bag must have shrunk overnight because my gear wouldn't all fit inside. There was no combination of packing the contents that allowed me to get a proper seal. Debi, who was watching me struggle, walked past me carrying her tightly sealed bag and said, "Sit on it."

She wasn't being rude. She was suggesting that I actually sit on the bag. It worked like a charm. All I had to do was put my weight on the bag and let the air squeeze out for a minute or two. As soon as I stood up, I quickly grabbed the bands at the top of the bag and rolled them a couple of times before air sucked back into the vacuum.

All I had left to pack were our sleeping kits. The pillows and sleeping bags were easy enough to put away; it was the tarp that was giving us trouble. Since the tarp gets shoved into the same bag as your pillow and sleeping bag, it's important to get the sand off of it. Flipping the tarp in the air a couple of times to get the dry sand off was easy. The difficult part was removing the wet sand. Moisture had accumulated on the underneath side of the tarp, and wet sand was sticking to it. You wouldn't think wet sand would be that hard to get off a vinyl tarp, but it is. That's why O.A.R.S. put "whisk broom" on the suggested packing list. It was maddening trying to get that sand off, but I finally learned a trick. When I draped the tarp over a shrub or tamarisk tree, both sides of the tarp were exposed to air and would dry in about twenty minutes. Then I could clean the sand off the tarp with a few good whips into the air.

Despite how long it took us to organize, take down and pack up in the mornings, we were never in a hurry. There was always time to leisurely eat breakfast, talk with the crew and other passengers, and poke around the area of our campsite. There are no clocks on the river. I left my wristwatch on out of habit, but there was no purpose for it. I could turn to Karen and say, "It's 8:00 am," but what would she do with that information? We had no set schedule, so it didn't matter what time it was.

The boatmen spoke about time in river units. When the crew was about finished breaking down camp and loading the boats, Eric said, "Let's all gather around the dories in five river units." That meant sometime shortly, although not necessarily five minutes.

Left to right: Mark, Betsy, Andrew, and Maia at the dishwashing station.

Debi getting the air out of her dry bag.

PREPARING FOR RAPIDS

Over the past day and a half, Eric had been teaching us about river life. His lessons came in waves rather than all at once. Five river units later it was time for the next set of instructions: how to survive the rapids.

The day before we got a small taste of white water on the river. (When I say "white water" I mean brown water. The churn of the river through the rapids was the color of foam on top of a double fudge hot chocolate.)

The Glen Canyon Dam controls the level of the Colorado River through the Grand Canyon. No longer does the river's flow spike during runoff season or slow to a trickle during the summer or times of severe drought. A multi-state treaty and the electricity demand from customers connected to the electricity grid in the Southwest determine the rate at which water is released from the dam.

Before the construction of the Glen Canyon Dam, the volume of water flowing through the river would normally peak at about 80,000 cfs in June, depending on snow melt and rainfall upstream. Now with the dam in place, flow rates have fluctuated between 8,000 cfs and 25,000 cfs in the past couple of decades. That's still a wide enough range to keep the boatmen downstream paying attention and adjusting their lines through the rapids accordingly. But it is not the same as being a wild, unpredictable river.

For anyone who hasn't much experience traveling on rivers (like me), the idea of cubic feet per second (cfs) is hard to understand in practical terms. I have no context for how much water a given number of cfs is. I tried to relate cfs to something I'm familiar with. For instance, I know how big a Home Depot bucket is: five gallons. A cubic foot of water is about seven and a half gallons. But neither of these facts is helpful when trying to comprehend 20,000 cfs. Several times on our trip a crewmember would tell us a story and would say something to the effect of, "...and the water was running at 20,000 cfs, can you believe that?" I had no idea what 20,000 cfs meant.

To give myself a more relatable comparison, I looked up the volume of a school bus, which is about 1,000 cubic feet. Not all school buses are the same size of course, but this gives you a rough idea of what 1,000 cubic feet looks like. Now, when someone tells you the river is running at 20,000 cfs, imagine twenty school buses driving past you in one second, except they're made of water, and another twenty are right behind them, and another twenty are behind them and so on.

Only once in the history of Glen Canyon Dam have the dam operators opened the floodgates to relieve pressure on the dam. They did this in 1983, causing the river's flow rate below the dam to jump to nearly 100,000 cfs. The National Park Service closed the river in the Grand Canyon during that release. Regardless, this rare event provided a singular, albeit illegal, opportunity for a group of extraordinarily enthusiastic boatmen to attempt to break the speed record for a boat trip down the river through the canyon.

Other than the 1983 intentional flood, there have only been a few times when flow rates coming out of the dam have been increased beyond the normal range. These controlled floods were for environmental purposes such as to determine if high flow rates could move enough sand to rebuild the disappearing beaches and sandbars along the river.

Even though the river is no longer wild, that doesn't mean it's tame. There are areas of the river that are quite calm and peaceful, yet according to my waterproof, tearproof *Grand Canyon Map and Guide* there are sixty-eight rapids of notable size in the canyon. Twenty-eight of those rapids are between Lees Ferry and Phantom Ranch.

Depending on the flow rate of the river, some of the rapids can be very dangerous, even deadly. People have died on the Colorado River in the Grand Canyon, but many of those deaths involved preventable factors such as not wearing a life jacket or other recommended safety gear, or going into the river while intoxicated.

The average speed of the river is about three and one-half miles per hour. Over the entire 277 miles, it drops on average about eight feet per mile. However, the rate of descent is about 100 feet per mile in the first twenty-five miles or so below Lees Ferry. With that fact remaining, the most challenging or dangerous rapids are not in the first twenty-five miles. In general, it's not the size of the drop that determines the difficulty of a rapid. Debris flows (rocks) from tributaries and side canyons are the cause of nearly every rapid on the river. Water passing over them creates waves and turbulence (rapids). The size and orientation of the underwater boulders determine a rapid's difficulty as well as the topography of the river at the site of the debris. A constriction in the river along with nasty debris beneath the surface is the recipe for a challenging rapid.

Contrary to what I thought previously, higher flow rates don't necessarily make a rapid more challenging to run. Depending on the rapid, a lower flow rate might increase its danger or difficulty. Each rapid has a unique signature, and boatmen with years of experience know the nuances of them all. Those who have seen the rapids in a variety of conditions have a better chance of having a golden run: a trip with no collisions or flips.

Eric stood on his dory and waited for all of the passengers to gather around. "Today we'll be going through some big rapids, so there are a few things you need to know," he began.

"First, let's talk about what to wear. The water can make you cold even on sunny days like today. There are a lot of places in the canyon where we'll be in the shade and you might get chilled. Rain gear is a good idea if you have it. You *will* get wet. Water shoes or those wet socks are also a good idea. Waves will come over the side of the boat and fill up the footwells where you'll be sitting, so your feet will be in water much of the time.

"We'll be wearing helmets for the first rapid this morning. You don't need to wear your helmets all day. Your boatman will decide on which rapids you'll need to wear them." I looked over, and Karen already had her helmet on.

"Also, remember what we talked about yesterday regarding your life jackets. They need to be tight enough so someone could pull you into the boat by the top of the jacket. Don't make it so tight you can't breathe, but it needs to be snug. If you wear rain gear, it needs to go under your life jacket, so you might have to adjust the straps for that extra bulk. Everybody with me so far?"

Everyone nodded, and Eric continued, "OK. So let's talk about what you should do if you become an involuntary swimmer."

Karen whispered to me, "What's an *involuntary* swimmer?"

"It's someone who's fallen out of the boat," I said.

"Then why didn't he say that?"

"Shhhh, this is the important part."

"Now you're in the water. It's no big deal; you have a life jacket on. It happens sometimes. What you want to do is to try to face the direction the river is flowing. So, try to float facing downstream. And try to keep your feet in front of you. This way if you hit a rock or something in the water, you'll hit it with your feet first instead of your head or back. OK?"

Karen whispered to me, "I don't want to be an

involuntary swimmer."

"No one does, that's why it's called involuntary."

Eric continued, "If you're in the water though, what you really want to do is get back in the boat as quickly as possible. Swim back to the boat if you can. But if you can't swim back to the boat you were in, try to swim to another boat, or raft, doesn't matter which. You just don't want to swim to shore. If you swim to shore and then all of the boats go past you we'll have a hard time getting to you. So, swim to a boat.

"Now, every boat has a bag like this." Eric held up what looked like a dry bag with a rope coming out of it. The bag was about the size of a one-gallon milk container. "This bag has a rope inside of it. One end of the rope is attached to the boat. If you are not too far away, we can throw this bag toward you. The rope comes out like this, you see? If we do that, then swim to the rope and we'll pull you back in. One thing to remember, try to listen to what the boatman is telling you to do. Stay calm and listen for the boatman. You'll be fine. We'll get you into a boat and you'll warm up and you'll have a fun story to tell."

I whispered to Karen, "Remember, do *not* swim to shore."

"Oh, I'm swimming to shore. You guys will just have to row back upstream to get me."

"Swim to a boat," I said. She shushed me.

"Everybody OK so far?" Eric asked. "Now, we'll be going through some rough water. All the boatmen have done these rapids before, but each time they are different. If the rapid is difficult, like House Rock we'll be running this morning, we'll stop and scout it first. Here, we can just hike up around the corner and see the rapids from shore. So, the boatmen and I will scout the rapids; you can come with us if you want. Then, we'll talk about it and decide on the best approach."

Eric paused for a moment to make sure we were all paying attention, and then continued. "Now, sometimes a wave catches us in a certain way, or something happens that causes the boat to flip over. We've all flipped before." He was referring to all of the boatmen. "It's no big deal, but we all need to know what to do if this happens."

Karen whispered, "They've all flipped before?"

"Shhh."

"If the boat you are in flips, stay calm. These dories have hatches that are watertight—or, watertight enough to hold air for a while—so they give the boat some buoyancy. It won't sink. Now the boat's upside down in the water, and all the passengers are in the water. If you happen to be stuck under the boat…"

Karen said, "I'm out."

"Listen," I said.

"If you happen to be stuck under the boat, don't worry. There's air under there. These footwells, when they're upside down, create air pockets. So you can hang out in there for awhile, no problem."

"No problem my ass," Karen whispered to me.

"If you happen to be under the boat when it's upside down, it'll be dark under there," he explained. "So, try to feel your way to the side. See the gunwales on both sides of the boat? Feel for one of those and push yourself under the gunwales and out. No problem. Now you're out from under the boat and hopefully with all your boat mates. On the underside of each dory is a safety line. Can you see it there? It's about at the waterline. That's what you hold onto if the boat is upside down. Try to grab the safety line and hold on. Remember, you want to try to stay with the boat.

"Now we're all out from underneath the boat, we're all holding onto the safety line, it's a beautiful sunny day, and we're taking a swim. But we all need to get to the same side of the boat so we can flip it back over."

Karen whispered to me, "So the boat flips, I'm stuck underneath it, I have to survive on the air in the footwell, then I have to swim out from underneath the boat in total darkness, swim back to the boat, grab the safety line and follow the safety line to the other side of the boat where everyone else is—all while we're being hurtled through white water?"

"Yes. Shhhh."

"We're all going to die."

"You won't be doing all of that in white water," I whispered. "By the time the air runs out in the footwell, we'll be in calmer water."

"Thank you. That was not helpful," she said.

Back to Eric, "These dories aren't easy to flip back over. What we do is, we all get up on the boat, which will be the bottom. And we grab the safety line on the other side of the boat and lean backward. It takes a lot of weight to do this so we have to really lean back. If we are successful, then we all fall back into the water, and the boat flips right side up. There you go. Then all we have to do is get back in the boat without flipping it over again. Everybody got that?"

Of course none of us "got" all of that, but we acted as if we did. What we did get was that this wasn't Splash Mountain at Disney World. Some serious stuff can happen on the river, and we needed to have some idea of what to do.

I asked, "How often do these boats flip?"

"You know, it happens. We all want to have a golden run, but sometimes the river has something else in mind. Don't worry; we're going to have a great day no matter what."

We were beginning to learn one of the unwritten and unspoken rules of the river: be positive, but be prepared. The boatmen were experienced and knew what to do if we got into a difficult spot, but all the talk was positive. It may be superstition, but whatever it was, they wouldn't even joke about flipping a boat, or hitting a rock, or a passenger going overboard.

Eric continued, "Alright, enough about that stuff. Let's talk about what you need to do when we go through the rapids. Yes, you. You play a big part of getting through the white water safely. Most importantly, you need to listen to what the boatman tells you and do what he asks. There are two things that you'll need to do: high side and bail. Let's talk about high siding first.

"We want to try to keep the boat as level as possible when

we go through rapids. It's crucial that you don't move around a lot when we are going through white water. Don't stand up or hang off the side of the boat. I know you guys wouldn't do that, but we've seen some crazy behavior on the river with some passengers.

"If the boat tips way to one side, the boatman can't get both oars in the water, so that's a problem. And if we tip too far we could flip. One way to keep that from happening is to use your weight to counteract the effect of a wave. So, when we approach a wave, especially a big one, we might yell, 'High side!' That means to lean into the wave. Your instinct may be to lean away; we all want to avoid danger so we back away from something we are afraid of, but in this case we want to do the opposite and lean into the wave. The bigger the wave, the more we need to lean into it. Got that? It's pretty simple; you'll do fine.

"The other thing that we'll need you to do is bail. These areas where your feet are resting will fill with water when waves come over the side of the boat. All of the boats have a couple of buckets in the front and back that you'll use for bailing. You're gonna want to bail anyway so your feet aren't sitting in freezing cold water, but there's a more important reason we need you to bail. That amount of water might not seem like a lot, but it is, and it's heavy. The heavier the boat is, the more effort it takes the boatman to maneuver it through the rapids. There are times we need to make some quick moves in the middle of the rapid, so the lighter we can make the boat the better. When the boatman yells, 'Bail,' he means it. We need you to bail as quickly as you can. That's really a big help."

Eric made sure we were prepared and that we appreciated the seriousness of what we were about to do, but he was calm during his safety talk. The crew still had cargo to load, and the boatmen needed to scout the rapids. This gave us time to get into our rain gear.

It seemed odd putting on so much gear on a warm sunny day. In addition to my hiking pants and shirt, I had on a rain jacket, rain pants, neoprene socks, and closed-toed water shoes, which were also suitable for hiking. Once Karen had her rain gear, life jacket and helmet on, she looked like a hazmat worker. The only parts of her body showing were her hands and a small opening around her face just big enough for her eyes, nose, and mouth.

Eric's safety talk unnerved Karen. I could sense that the part about surviving on the air trapped in the footwells put her over the edge. Most people from our generation remember the movie *The Poseidon Adventure*, the original 1972 version. We were still kids when it was a big hit. Karen must have thought that we were about to star in a real-life version: the boat capsizes, and Eric has to lead us to the bow so we can escape through the hole rescuers have cut in the bottom of the dory. I can still remember Gene Hackman's character imploring the passengers as they headed toward the engine room, "You're going the wrong way, damn it!"

The other passengers were poking fun at Karen, but she didn't care. She was prepared for the worst. She gave a little wave to the group and said, "If I don't make it through House Rock Rapid, please tell my unborn grandchild Clara that even though Mimi never got to meet her, she loved her very much." Spoiler alert: Karen made it through just fine and met Clara a month later.

Eric giving us the safety talk before our first big rapid of the trip.

Karen and Lolly, all bundled up and ready to go.

FIRST RAPID

John and I climbed into the passenger seats at the bow of Andy's boat. We enjoyed riding with Andy so much we asked him again on the second day if we could be his passengers. Lolly and Karen were in the back with their arms around each other. I don't mean they had their arms around the other's shoulders like they were posing for a photo; they had both arms wrapped like the boogeyman was about to get them. Andy glanced back at them, smiled and shook his head as he pushed his dory away from shore.

I say "push" because that's how the boatmen propel their dories, by pushing on the oars rather than the traditional technique of pulling on the oars. According to Powell's diary of his expeditions, his men rowed in the traditional method of the rower facing backward; they had to look over their shoulders from time to time to see where they were going. Today, dory boatmen face downriver. There's a practical reason why this is the preferred method: it lets them see where they're going. On flat water, it's fine for the rower to look back in his direction of travel every so often, but in the Grand Canyon, the boatman needs to face the rapids so he or she can make quick adjustments.

There wasn't much time for Lolly and Karen to fret about the white water. It seemed like we'd just yelled, "Ho!" when

Eric's boat dropped into House Rock Rapid. Eric always went into a rapid first. Most of the time, when we got within a hundred yards or so of a rapid, he would stand in the center of his dory to get a better look at what was ahead. Eric would study the water while his boat drifted toward the drop-off. When he had seen enough, he would sit back down and make his final approach. The other boatmen hung back and took their lead from Eric.

Eric's dory bobbed and twisted through the water. We could hear screams and laughter from the passengers in his dory. Then the next boat dropped in. Waves came over their bow and the sides of the boat. I could tell we were going to get wet, like jumping into the deep end wet. Ours was the last dory to go through the rapid. Behind us were the support rafts; they always followed the dories. I'm sure it wasn't easy for the boatmen of the support rafts to get through the rapids safely, but the rafts are more forgiving when it comes to hitting rocks. Their margin of error is greater.

When the other three dories had entered the rapid, I looked at Andy; he was calm, almost too calm I thought. Through the course of the day though, we learned that Andy knew what he was doing. Not only was he a skilled boatman with decades of experience, but he also knew his old boat, the *Cottonwood*, like it was an extension of his body. About thirty yards or so from the rapid Andy said to me, "Hey, Matt, could you move to your left a couple of inches?" I scooted over, and he mouthed, "Perfect." He was fine-tuning the balance of the boat. Then he turned the dory sideways; we were going in perpendicular to the shore.

As confident and in control as Andy was, the river had us in its grasp. Once you're past the point of no return, the currents and waves take over. I'll always remember the sensation of the rapids drawing the boat in. It's similar to the feeling on a roller coaster when the cars reach the top of an incline and the click, click, click of the conveyor ends. The roller coaster pauses for a moment and then glides over the edge. Instead of a long free fall though, an explosion of waves abruptly interrupted our drop.

We had a couple of places to hold onto to keep from falling out. The gunwales, the top of the sides of the boats, are made for gripping. And at the front of the footwells, about knee height, are handholds as well. I had one hand on the gunwale and one hand on the bar in front of me.

As the first wave came over the top of John's side of the boat, John and I quickly leaned into it; the wave engulfed us both. All the air went out of my lungs as I gasped. The rain gear was useless. In fact, for a brief moment, my rain pants became balloons filled with water. Not only was the rain gear not keeping me dry, but it was also holding the water in close to my body. The footwell instantly filled and our legs were sitting in a foot and a half of 48-degree water.

Lolly and Karen were laughing uncontrollably. "Getting wet up there?" they yelled. I looked back and saw them sitting high above Andy, dry as a bone. They were way above the rest of us because the boat was diving into the next wave. With what seemed like the flick of an oar, Andy pulled the boat back parallel to the shore. As we headed into the next wave face first, John and I disappeared under water. Thankfully, when we came up, we were still in our seats. All we could hear was the roar of the water and the women laughing.

In less than a couple of minutes from when it started, we were peacefully floating on flat water. "Folks, it's time to bail," Andy said. At our feet were a couple of plastic containers with the bottoms cut off. Mine used to be a radiator fluid container, and John's was an old milk carton. They were attached to the boat with a thin rope. John and I got all but the last inch of water out of our footwell in short order. "How's it going back there?" Andy asked. He must have been able to tell by how the *Cottonwood* was riding that the back footwell was still filled with water.

Karen said, "Andy, I think our bailing things are broken." We all looked back to see Karen holding her plastic milk jug in one hand and its lid in the other. She thought that she was supposed to fill the container through the top, which of course would be impossible because the bottom had been cut out. Lolly added, "Yeah, mine has a big hole in it. And I can't get the lid off." Andy, John and I laughed so hard we couldn't speak. While we were laughing, I could see Karen and Lolly whispering to each other. Lolly said, "Oh, I get it," then Karen screwed the lid back onto her container. I couldn't wait until we got to shore to tell the others.

The bailing container humiliation didn't keep the wives from ribbing us about getting wet. "You guys look like a couple of drowned rats!" laughed Lolly.

John asked, "Andy, how is it that those of us in the front of the boat went completely under a couple of times and those in the back are completely dry?" Andy smiled and shrugged his shoulders oh so slightly, and then winked at us. The wives didn't see the wink. John and I interpreted Andy's sign as meaning, "The day's not over yet."

"It's nice and warm back here. You guys cold up there?" Karen asked.

"Go ahead, dig the hole deeper," I thought.

Lolly said mockingly, "I don't think I needed my rain gear for that. I'm kind of hot now."

It was getting warm and I was sitting in the boat with my black rain pants on and my thighs in the sun. We froze when we went through the rapids, but now on flat water my legs got hot quickly in the direct sunlight. I dipped my bandana over the side of the boat and then squeezed the river water on my thighs to cool them off.

"Andy, I bet you have a lot of stories about difficult passengers, don't you?" I asked. I was baiting him to say, "Not as bad as those two in the back," but he didn't.

"No, not many. Most people who come on this trip are pretty good to be around," he replied.

Andy seemed like someone who would be friends with everyone he met. He wasn't about to dig up dirt on past passengers.

"There was this one couple though," he started. "They

came on this trip in hopes of patching up their marriage. So, instead of marriage counseling, they decided to spend two weeks on the river. On top of that, they were also smokers and had decided that this trip would be a good time to quit smoking, cold turkey. They were difficult passengers. We had to keep them from killing each other."

"So, what happened?" I asked.

"I'll just say they didn't make it."

"What do you mean they didn't make it?"

"We had to have them helicoptered out of the canyon mid-way through the trip."

I looked at Lolly and said, "See, Andy can have you outta here if you cause too much trouble."

"I don't think I'm the one they'll be putting on the helicopter, Matt," she replied.

Left to right: Lolly, Karen (taking picture), Andy, Matt and John on the *Cottonwood*

Lolly, Wendy and Rachel

AFTERNOON ON THE RIVER

Three miles past House Rock Rapid, we saw Eric angling toward the right-hand bank of the river. "Here you go, Lolly. Eric called in a helicopter to take you out. Laughing at other passengers won't be tolerated," I said. We were pulling over for a mid-morning hike just short of mile 21.

I was glad to be able to peel off all of the gear we were wearing: rain pants, rain jacket, life jacket, and helmet. Standing on the beach in just our hiking clothes, it felt like summer again. Maia hauled a five-gallon jug of drinking water off her raft and set it on the sand next to a container of Gatorade powder. We spent the next five or ten minutes filling our water bottles and putting on sunscreen.

"Who wants to go for a hike?" Eric asked.

Participating in the day hikes was optional, but he knew the answer before he asked the question. All twenty-six of us were going on the hike. Another responsibility of the trip leader is to assess the passengers' physical abilities, and plan each day accordingly. The leader doesn't want to take a group on an activity that they're not capable of doing; that's not fun for anyone. Eric had been observing us to determine whether we could do the hike up North Canyon. Apparently, we passed the test because we all took off in a single-file line heading up the canyon.

The weather that morning was perfect: sunny and low 70s. For the first half of a mile or so we hiked through a flat wash in full sun toward the side canyon. As the canyon narrowed, we began climbing up stair step rocks in the shade. The elevation gain was gradual; I would rate the hike as moderately difficult. We didn't know at the time the name of the area in which we were hiking. Later, I learned it was North Canyon. We'd beached the boats just shy of the North Canyon Rapids.

The payoff for the hike was a stunning sight: a small pour-off, with a trickle of a stream running down the center into a shallow pool of water. Since the walls of the canyon were close to one another at that point, there was no wind. The pool was flat as glass and the reflection of the blue sky and red canyon walls was exquisite.

Karen and I didn't bring a camera on the trip. We both intended to use our phones. We'd found on recent trips that the photos taken with our phones looked better than the ones taken with our dedicated cameras, so we stopped bringing them on trips. However, in the canyon, my phone kept freezing on me. There would be hour-long periods when I couldn't get it to turn on. As a result, at times Karen was our sole family photographer.

About five years earlier, when we were traveling to all of the national parks, I'd started a Photo of the Day Contest. I was the only contestant and also the judge. Each day I would look through my pictures and vote on the photo of the day. Karen had a grand time making fun of me when she learned of my secret contest; it provided her with a couple of years of humor. Then one day when we were on a trip, she asked me, "Which of my photos do you like for the photo of the day?"

"The what?"

"The photo of the day. I'm trying to decide on today's winner."

"Hold up! You are not part of the Photo of the Day Contest. I thought I made it clear that there is a formal acceptance process and you have not yet been accepted into the program. Your application is still under review."

"Why?"

"First, you made fun of the contest and have not shown enough remorse for doing so. And second—there's no second—you haven't been accepted yet."

After that day she groveled enough to get accepted into the program and is now one of the judges, but I don't think she's objective in her voting. She has never cast a vote for one of my photos.

Karen took a bunch of pictures of the pour-off. Each one was incredible. She showed them to me on her phone. "Dang it!" I thought to myself, "It's a Sasquatch day." A Sasquatch day is when one of us has taken such a great photo that the other pretty much needs to take a picture of a Sasquatch to win that day's Photo of the Day Contest. "Good luck finding a Sasquatch, that is, if you ever get your phone working," she said to me. This is the attitude that kept her from being accepted into the contest in the first place.

We all sat on the rocks close to the small pool of water and snacked on nuts and trail mix. From where we were sitting we couldn't see beyond the top of the pour-off, but it looked like the trail might continue.

One of the passengers asked Eric, "Is there a trail up there?"

"Yeah, it goes a little further past the stream."

Paul said, "Well, then I'm going in." He took off his pack and shirt and started wading through the pool. I've waded through greener pools of stagnant water, but I wasn't about to follow him. We all cheered him on, "Go Paul, go Paul, go Paul." He tried as hard as he could to keep his mid-section above the water, but eventually, he had to dog paddle to reach the other side. By the time he made it across, several of the women had begun stripping down to their bathing suits and following him.

Andrew thought that he might be able to climb around the pool to the other side. The pool was about fifty feet wide and a little longer than that. The smooth rock walls on both sides were nearly vertical, but Andrew thought that maybe, just maybe he could do it. He started out wearing his flip-flops but quickly switched to bare feet. He looked like Spiderman clinging to the wall. Several times we thought he would fall, but then he would catch himself. It was a good five minutes of entertainment. About half way across he was stuck: no way to go forward, no way to back up. He knew what he had to do: the old Nestea plunge backward into the water.

Given his age and fitness, Andrew had the best chance of any of us to climb around the pool without falling in. This fact didn't stop a couple of the other male passengers from giving it a shot, each try ending the same way. It was a fun show, but I'm glad I stayed dry.

It was still too early for lunch when we got back to the boats, so Eric decided we would make our way further down the river before stopping to eat. He suggested that we wear our helmets again, rain gear was optional. With a "Dories, Ho!" we were off and into the Roaring Twenties: a section of the river between miles 20 and 27 that has eight named rapids.

Our experience with the next rapid we ran was similar to House Rock, except it was my turn to be smacked with a big wave. Boy, that first one is cold, especially after hiking in the warm sun. The gals in back picked up where they had left off. "You look a little wet, Matt," Lolly said. Karen giggled uncontrollably. I looked back at Andy and gave him a look that said, "I think it's time for those gals to get taken down a notch or two." Andy smiled and said, "You have to lean into those big waves. Like you're going to give them a big kiss."

"Yeah, you have to kiss those waves, Matt," Lolly added. Then she and Karen burst into laughter.

By the third or fourth rapid we were familiar with Andy's approach. Rarely did he go into a rapid exactly parallel to the shore. He knew each rapid and precisely the best way to enter. So it wasn't surprising when we approached the next rapid nearly in reverse, one that had a ominously large first wave. I knew what was coming: even though Lolly was in the back, she was heading straight into the Big Kahuna.

The back of the dory went under the wave, then just as quickly shot straight up. I could see Karen and Lolly above us and was a little surprised they didn't fly out of the boat. Lolly was drenched and gasping for air. Thirty seconds later we were back on flat water. "Bail!" Andy yelled.

"Our footwell is bone dry, Andy," I yelled back. "You look at little wet, Lolly. And what happened to your sunglasses?" She was fishing them out of the footwell as she bailed.

"I kissed that mother, Andy!" Lolly yelled. That brought a laugh from our boatman. "She kissed that mother," he chuckled. "I haven't heard anyone say that in my dory before." (I censored the passage above, like I usually do with everything John and Lolly say, but I think you get the gist of her exchange with Andy.)

The Roaring Twenties were great fun. Everyone got his or her turn at being the drowned rat. Somewhere in the middle of them, I don't know for sure which mile of the river, we stopped for lunch.

Having guided trips through the canyon many times before, Eric knew exactly the spot where he wanted to land for lunch. He slid his dory onto a beach, and the other boatmen parked their boats next to his. Each time we made it to shore, the beaches were a little less muddy. It hadn't rained again upstream since the night before we got on the river. The mud that the Paria was pumping into the Colorado River was tapering off, and there was less silt to settle on shore. The going ashore routine was the same each time: take the life jacket off and latch it to the side of the boat, same with helmets if you were wearing one, find your daypack and water bottle inside the hatch and awkwardly clamor across the deck of the dory and over the side. Hopefully, you can step onto the shore or at least into water shallow enough so as not to submerge your body too deep into the frigid water.

Within the time it took us to find a spot to set down our bags, lay our wet clothes on a sunny rock, and climb back on the dory to retrieve the things we'd forgotten to bring ashore, the crew had set up a table to prepare lunch. They had also erected a serving table and a hand washing station.

We got an orientation on how lunch is done on the river since this was our first full day on the water. Eric was quick to give us a few instructions because he could tell that once we saw the crew unwrap packages of food, there was a good chance we would overwhelm the serving table and self-serve our way into complete chaos.

"OK, everybody," he began. "The crew will prepare lunch, but we have a few rules. When we're fixing lunch, we need everyone to stay away from the prep table. We've done this many times before and we know what we're doing. But we are in close contact and there are knives flying. If anyone sticks their hand in the prep area before we finish, they could lose a finger. In the meantime, you all need to wash your hands. Our lunches are always finger food, so everyone needs to wash up—no exceptions."

I turned to Karen and whispered, "Finger food? What is finger food?"

"I think he means that we eat everything with our hands, like sandwiches."

Eric continued, "I know everyone is hungry so we put out snacks on the serving table you can munch on until we are ready."

On the serving table was a small pile of apple slices, a jar of peanut butter and one unopened container of Pringles potato chips. Now, I don't want this to sound like a complaint, it's just an observation: if you read the side of a Pringles can, you will learn that there are approximately eighty potato chips per container. There were twenty-six people in our party. Split evenly, each person would be allotted three potato chips, with two lucky persons getting a bonus, fourth chip.

Here's the thing about Pringles when you're hungry: it's as if the first few chips you eat don't even touch your mouth. They vaporize just as you begin to crunch down on them, especially when you're famished. It takes a lot of willpower to not automatically rapid fire them into your mouth. You don't get a sense that you're eating anything at all until about the seventh or eighth chip. I'm sure Karen and I have eaten an entire container of Pringles between the two of us as a snack after a long hike.

To see the group contemplating how they would politely share the potato chips and make them last ten minutes was a little frightening. I knew immediately that it was a bad idea for me to eat a single chip. If I had, the trip would have been over, at least for me. I would have eaten one, then another, then taken the entire container and made a run for it. Later, after the angry passengers and crew tracked me down, they would stake me to a rock close to the river with all of my belongings. They would put a cardboard sign around my neck with the words "FOOD HOARDER!" on it and leave me there. If I were lucky, another group would find me and tow me in an inner tube to Phantom Ranch where they would then turn me over to the National Park Service.

Instead, I grabbed a couple of apple slices and went in search of shade.

Lunch consisted of make-your-own cold cut sandwiches. There were no plates, so there were no dishes to clean afterward. Micro trash wasn't a problem either; we were so hungry that the crumbs never made it to the ground. JB told us a story of a trip he was on in the early days with Martin Litton. Somehow the sandwich bread they brought on the trip got wet, and the crew had to lay all of the slices in the sun to dry. The bread then crumbled when they put it back in bags. Martin was unfazed. The next day he announced that they were having "handwiches" for lunch. Everyone was to take a handful of breadcrumbs and then place the meat and cheese on top. Handwiches, problem solved.

The crew placed a couple of packages of cookies on the serving table for dessert: Oreos and Pecan Sandies. Sandies for dessert, how appropriate. Again I fought the urge to grab the entire package of Oreos; I love Oreos. I was able to control myself and take only one cookie, but if they ever put out both the Pringles and Oreos at the same time, I might make my move.

Most of the time we imagined that no one else was on the river but us. Once or twice a day we would see another party float by. While we were eating lunch, a group of kayakers passed us. There was a rapid just downstream from our lunch site, and I had a good view of them running it. Once in the rapid, it didn't appear as if they had much control of what happened next: choose your entry point and then hold on. One of them flipped while we were watching, but he righted himself before drifting out of sight.

Back on the river, we had several rapids left to go before stopping for the night. On the flat sections of the river I pressed Andy for more passenger stories, "Andy, you must have some other wild stories about passengers to share with us."

"The most unusual group was on the very first trip I worked as a boatman," he said. "There was a British guy and a French guy, and they hated each other. One night we were setting up for dinner, and we heard them yelling at each other. When we got to them the British guy had the French guy by the collar. He was holding him up against a boulder yelling, 'I'm going to kill you!' They were something. We had to keep them apart for the entire trip."

"Why did they hate each other?" I asked.

"We could never figure that out. They both had strong personalities, and they rubbed each other the wrong way. The British fellow loved to tell stories. One morning a few of us were standing around the breakfast area, and the Brit was in the middle of one of his stories. The French guy approached us; he was carrying a razor, shaving cream, and a mirror. He had a towel neatly folded across his forearm; he was headed to the river for a proper morning shave. Well, he pushed through our group on his way to the river. He didn't say anything, just walked between us. So, we watched as he started shaving at the riverbank, dipping his razor in the water and carefully watching himself in his mirror. The Brit said, 'Excuse me for a moment gents,' and walked to the river. He stood a few feet upstream from where the French guy was shaving and proceeded to pee in the river. That's the kind of stuff we had to deal with the entire trip."

"Andy, I have another question for you. You've guided trips on a lot of rivers. If *you* were to go on a river trip, as a passenger, and you could only choose one river, which would it be? And your answer can't be the Colorado River through the Grand Canyon."

"Hmmm, one river? I'd have to say the Middle Fork."

"Is that the name of the river? Middle Fork?"

"The Middle Fork of the Salmon River."

"OK, in Idaho?"

"Yep, I think that would be my choice."

During the week, we rode with each of the four dory boatmen. I asked all of them the same question while we were on the river so none of them could hear the others' answers. All four said the same thing: Middle Fork. We might have to check that out in the future.

At mile 33 we could see Eric in the lead dory heading toward shore. He was parking his boat on a wide, white sand beach at the mouth of a huge rock overhang, Redwall Cavern. The cavern sits on the outside bank of a sharp bend in the river. The rock wall along the bank is Redwall Limestone. Over countless years, the river has flooded and raced around this bend. In doing so, it carved an opening in the limestone. Closest to the shore, the roof of the cavern looked to be about 75 to 100 feet above the sandy floor. We could easily walk back into the cavern for about 100 yards. The opening was as deep as it was wide.

John Wesley Powell described the cavern as large enough that it "would give sitting to 50,000 people." It's hard to say if that's an accurate estimation. I'd guess you could fit one-fifth that many people inside the cavern, but it would get a little stuffy. The ceiling is high enough that it never felt claustrophobic. It does make you wonder though what keeps the entire thing from collapsing. I think about this a lot when I'm under rock overhangs and in caves. I asked a ranger at Carlsbad Caverns National Park years ago, what is it that keeps the ceiling of rock openings from falling. He said, "The arch of the roof gives the opening its main support. The arch is the strongest shape in nature. That's what allows most caves to exist without collapsing for millions of years." The roof of Redwall Cavern had a smooth, wide, arched shape, which gave me comfort.

On a rainy day, a river group could hang out in Redwall Cavern and stay dry. The large, wide-open space made me wish we'd brought a Frisbee with us on the trip. Standing at the back of the cavern I took some interesting photos looking toward the beach. The sun was dazzling as it shone on the river yet it was dim inside the cavern. When I positioned the camera on my phone just right, I was able to capture a stunning contrast of the light and dark.

Matt and Karen at North Canyon pour-off.

In North Canyon. Left to right: Matt, Bart, Joe, Karen (below), Paul, Maia, Andrew. Andrew is looking at the wall and thinking about trying to climb around the pool.

Andrew attempting to climb around the pool below the pour-off in North Canyon.

LITTLE REDWALL CAMP

According to the river clock, it was time to get to our campsite for the evening. The last boat ride of the day was a short one. Little Redwall, where we stopped for the night, was a mere one mile downriver. The site was smaller than our previous day's site. A high rock cliff about a hundred feet or so from the river was our backstop. We set up camp in the thin strip of sand between the cliff and the river. At Hot Na Na, all of the couples spread out across the beach with plenty of room between each tent. At Little Redwall, we decided to place our sleeping areas next to each other in a row. There was plenty of room, so we left 10-15 feet between each couple. It was like a slumber party in someone's backyard.

As we dragged our sleeping kits and pads toward the wall and found a place to settle, Karen looked worried. "I don't know about this sleeping without a tent idea," she said. "What if something bites me in the middle of the night?"

"What 'something' are you worried about?" I asked.

"Mouse, tarantula, scorpion, snake—take your pick. And those ringtail things, they're creepy."

I knew better than to take a drink of beer right after I asked her that question, but I did anyway. As soon as I stopped coughing and caught my breath, I did my best to ease her concerns.

"A mouse? You're worried that a mouse might bite you?"

"Yes! They have rabies!"

"A mouse isn't interested in biting people. All it wants to do is find something to eat, have sex and not get eaten by another animal."

"We're talking about a mouse now, not you," Karen said.

"My point is, Sweetie, that it's not going to take a bite out of you. It knows you are too big to eat."

"Too big to eat? Would you like to re-phrase that?"

"You know what I mean. Besides, they're more afraid of you than you are of them."

(In all seriousness, rodents can be a problem in the canyon, especially along the corridor of trails from the South Rim to the North Rim. The National Park Service advises campers to keep food in animal-proof containers. They also suggest not to hang food in trees or keep food in packs because rodents can still get to it. Outside that corridor of trails, mice are not a big concern. It's still wise to keep food in animal-proof containers wherever camping.)

Karen continued, "I read on the Internet that you have to watch out for ring-tailed cats when camping in the desert."

"There are cats down here?" I asked.

"They're not real cats. They just kind of look like cats. They're more like raccoons. The article said they are 'sleek and cunning.' I don't want anything sleek and cunning sniffing me in the middle of the night."

"Well, if they're cats, they'll take care of your mouse problem."

Ring-tailed cats are also known as "miner's cats" because miners used to keep them as pets so they would rid their camp of vermin. One article I read said that it wasn't so much that the miners domesticated the ring-tailed cats as the ring-tailed cats domesticated the miners.

"How about a scorpion? A scorpion could bite us in the middle of the night," Karen said.

I replied, "Scorpions don't bite, they sting," but I realized this wasn't helpful after I had said it. "Besides, if there are any scorpions around here they'll be more afraid of you than you are of them." People always use this phrase when they want someone else to stop worrying about a particular pest. How does anyone know this to be true? I thought to myself, "What if scorpions aren't afraid of anything? What if they enjoy a good fight and crawl around at night looking for trouble? If I were a scorpion, I might do just that."

"OK, a snake. A snake might bite me. It could bite *you* just as easily; you should be worried too."

"Snakes? You're worried about snakes?" I said with a confident snicker. "Snakes won't bother us. Besides, they're more afraid of you than you are of them." Karen wasn't buying any of it.

She said, "I heard about a river guide who brought her mother with her on a trip like this. Her mom laid their sleeping bags out a couple of hours before they went to bed. Later, when the river guide got into her sleeping bag, she could feel a large snake moving inside the bag down by her feet. She knew enough not to panic, and she let the snake slowly crawl across her body and out of the sleeping bag. She saw the rattle as it slid across her neck. What if that happens?"

I vigorously shook out my sleeping bag and went to find where the crew stacked the tents, just in case we changed our minds later. But I told Karen I was going for another beer.

Karen's concerns about mice were well-founded. A couple of years prior, we spent a few days on a houseboat with our friends Ben and Brittney and their extended family. Ben's houseboat was docked on Lake Powell, about seventy-five miles upstream from Little Redwall. There were five couples and seven young kids on the boat.

One of the highlights of the experience was sleeping on the top deck of the boat. We laid pads down on the deck—

similar to the Paco pads we used on the river—and slept under the stars. The first night we were awake for hours watching for shooting stars and contemplating the Milky Way. Bats flew above us, clearing the night sky of insects. Karen loved it; we both did.

The next morning while we were having breakfast, Ben said to Karen, "There's a mouse on the boat."

"A mouse! How do you know?" she asked.

"I've seen him. And I'm going to get him."

"How are you going to get him?"

"I have these glue blocks that I put around the boat at night. When the mouse steps on it, he's stuck."

"Then what? You have a live mouse stuck to the block?"

"No. They're always dead when I find them. I think they wear themselves out trying to get unstuck." Karen shuddered, she hates mice.

The third morning on the boat, Ben and I were having coffee on the back deck. The night before, the toddlers didn't sleep well, which meant none of us did. Two of them cried for hours, but they were now sleeping soundly. Karen, Ben and I were the only ones awake, and we were trying to stay quiet so we wouldn't wake anyone.

Karen was inside the cabin about twenty feet from Ben and me. There was a cubbyhole in the hallway of the cabin where Karen and I had stowed our clothes and personal stuff. Karen was standing barefoot in front of the cubby sorting through her clothes. She was choosing her outfit for the day.

While we were sitting there, Ben whispered to me slowly, "Matt." It was a creepy whisper.

I looked at him and whispered back in a creepy voice, "Yes."

He was staring at Karen. He said softly, "Do you see what I see?"

I looked in Karen's direction. "Oh no. No. No. No," I said quietly.

We were both frozen. Karen looked back at us. We didn't say a word. Our eyes were wide, and our mouths were half open. Karen smiled at us and began brushing her hair.

I did my best ventriloquist act and said to Ben. "Don't—say—a word." Ben was still frozen. Another minute passed, and I said softly without moving my lips, "Why did you put it *there?*" He didn't respond. We both sat staring at Karen.

Karen looked at us and asked in a playful tone, "What are you two up to?" We both shook our heads slowly back and forth.

At Karen's feet was one of Ben's glue blocks. It was black and about the size of a three-by-five index card. Karen's foot was grazing the side of the block. On top of the block was a big, dead, stuck mouse. I thought to myself, "If she steps on that block, all hell will break loose." I was imagining her running around the boat screaming with that glue block stuck to the bottom of her foot and a dead mouse sandwiched between the block and her foot. She might die trying to get it off, just like the mouse did. She very well could end up in the lake.

Without saying it to each other, we both knew that if we told Karen about the mouse, she would likely step on the block in her panic to get away from it. From our vantage point it looked like she was already touching it with the side of her foot. Ben said to her, "Hey, Karen. Can you come out here? I want to show you something."

"I want to show you something? Is that the best you got?" I whispered to him.

"I'll be there in a minute," Karen replied.

It was my turn. "Sweetie, can you do us a favor and bring the coffee out here? We need a refill." This was risky. Karen's usual response when I say something like that is to put one hand on her cocked hip and say, "Are your legs broken?" Or (my favorite), "Why don't you refill *this?*" But she didn't. Miraculously, she immediately turned and walked into the kitchen without sassing me.

She came out with the coffee pot and asked, "What did you want to show me, Ben?"

"Yeah, what did you want to show her, Ben?" I added.

"Uh, I was thinking. Well. Matt and I were talking, and I thought. Let me show you on the map here," he said.

There was a map of Lake Powell on the wall just inside the cabin. Ben led Karen to the map and said, "I thought that we might go to Rainbow Bridge today. Here's where we are, and there's Rainbow Bridge. Matt, why don't you show her, I have to go to the bathroom."

While I was fake-planning our trip to Rainbow Bridge with Karen, Ben silently grabbed the block and put it in a trash bag without Karen seeing it. Nothing good would have come from telling her about the mouse.

That night, as we were standing on the back of the boat about to climb to the top deck to go to bed, Karen shouted, "A mouse! Ben, there's your mouse!"

Ben and I came over to see where Karen was pointing. "Look! There he is! He's on the rope." The houseboat was tied to the shore with four long ropes, each at least an inch thick. Two stretched from the back of the boat up the rocky shore and were tied to large boulders. The other two were attached to the middle of the boat and secured to boulders lower on the shore. Ben had made sure the boat wasn't going anywhere if the wind picked up.

He grabbed a flashlight from the cabin and lit up the rope. Karen gasped. Ben sounded like a little kid when he yelled, "Look at 'em all!" He scanned each of the ropes with his flashlight. There were at least a couple of mice on every rope.

"Oh my God! The ropes are mouse highways!" Karen yelled. By now all of the other adults and children were hanging over the rail of the top deck watching. The kids squealed.

Ben banged on the ropes. The mice that didn't fall off ran the other direction. "We need to do something about this," I said tilting my head toward Karen. "Or no one will be sleeping tonight."

Given the amount of beer we'd drunk that evening, I'm surprised how quickly we devised a plan to keep the mice off the boat. Untying the boat wasn't an option. Well, it was, but we hadn't had that much to drink. Instead, we took a paper plate and cut a slit in it, and then cut a hole in the center of the plate the same diameter as the ropes. We slid the paper plate onto the rope a few feet away from the boat to block the mice. The plates looked like little satellite TV dishes with a rope going through the center. We put them on all of the ropes and stood at the back of the boat shining lights on them. We watched as the mice went right up to the plates and then turned around. It seemed to be working.

With the excitement over it was time for bed. Before we had a chance to turn away, a mouse ran across the handrail in front of us. One must have slipped through the gauntlet before we got the paper plates in place. Karen ran inside the cabin.

Ben yelled, "I'll get my gun!"

He turned to follow Karen into the cabin, but when he got to the doorway he hit an invisible barrier with his face. He fell to the deck. Karen had shut the sliding glass door behind her. I laughed so hard I thought I would pass out. Ben was laughing too. He tried to open the door, but Karen had locked it. "Karen, let me in!" he said.

She was face to face with him; they were a foot apart with the glass between them. She wouldn't open the door. She shook her head and yelled through the door, "No, I'm sorry Ben, but if I open the door the mouse will come in."

"Karen, you have to let Ben in," I pleaded, but she just kept shaking her head.

Ben was holding his face and laughing. Karen finally opened the door and ran to the center of the cabin. Ben unlocked the cabinet where he kept his pellet gun, and the hunt was on. He was holding the gun like Elmer Fudd held his gun in the Bugs Bunny cartoons. "He's got to be around here somewhere," he said.

We moved the table and chairs. We looked behind the icebox on the deck. We searched everywhere, but no mouse. For no good reason, I decided to open the lid to the barbecue. "There he is, on the grill!" Ben said. He aimed the gun, and I shouted, "Let me get out of the way first!" Ben's father-in-law was watching from the top deck and yelled, "Not on the grill!"

Ben fired the gun anyway. It was a direct hit; the dead mouse was laying where my hamburger had been a couple of hours earlier.

"That's it. I'm never eating at one of your barbecues ever again," I said.

Ben was holding his bicep and laughing. "What now?" I asked.

"The pellet ricocheted and hit me in the arm. It really hurts."

"Put the gun away," I said. "On second thought, we need to put the gun somewhere you can't find it."

That was Karen's Lake Powell mouseboat experience. Despite her concerns, she agreed to forego the tent that night, as did all of the other couples except Mark and Rachel. What helped give Karen the confidence to sleep outside was knowing that everyone else in the group would be sleeping close by. "There's safety in numbers," she said.

Our sleeping area was a raised bed of sand about 15 feet above the river. It was large enough for everyone to spread out their tarps and sleeping pads and store their dry bags. A day full of running rapids is a good test for whether you properly sealed your dry bag. At the end of the day, the cargo rafts looked like they had been through a truck wash. I failed the test; everything in the top half of my bag was dripping when I opened it. That's when I understood the importance of putting my stuff in Ziploc bags. None of my clothes were wet, just the outsides of the freezer bags.

At river level, the crew had enough space to set up the food preparation and serving tables, and the chair circle. I wandered down there to fill our water bottles. The five-gallon jug of drinking water was full. I asked one of the crew, "How much drinking water did you guys bring?"

"We didn't bring any. Other than what was in the jugs when we left Lees Ferry."

"Then where did this water come from?" I asked.

"From the river."

"From that river?" I asked as I pointed to the Colorado, which looked like the chocolate river flowing through Willy Wonka's factory.

"Yep. We fill a couple of five-gallon buckets with river water and then let them sit so the sediment settles to the bottom. Then we decant the clear water off the top, filter it, and treat it with chlorine tablets."

I had been drinking river water all day and didn't know it. It tasted fine, but I added some Gatorade powder to my water bottle for good measure.

The main item for dinner was grilled chicken. As soon as the male passengers saw the crew light the charcoal and unwrap the chicken breasts, they volunteered for grilling duty. What else would you expect when there's a bunch of guys standing around with all the beer they can drink, fire and meat? The more guys who tried to help, the greater the risk became that we would have chicken briquettes for dinner.

"I think the grate is too close to the fire."

"I just lowered it because it was too high."

"Are the ones on this side cooking faster than those over there?"

"I think they need to be flipped."

"No, I just flipped them. Go have another beer—and get me one while you're at it."

"Maybe we should pour beer on the fire to cool it down."

"Hey, don't touch that unless you washed your hands."

"I washed them this morning."

"OK, good."

"Maybe we should pour beer on the chicken."

"Which one is the one that we dropped in the sand?"

"It's that one there."

"No, that's the one that fell into the fire."

"How do you get sand off a chicken breast?"

"Is that the start of a bad joke?"

"No, seriously."

"Seriously, we should make sure these are cooked all the way. I don't want to die."

This went on for what seemed like way longer than it should take to cook twenty-six chicken breasts. It was a small miracle that we ate dinner that night.

The intimate setting of our campsite was the perfect spot for our second campfire of the trip. Rondo placed a fire mat on the sand in the center of the chair circle, and two crewmembers carefully carried the coal box from the grill and placed it on the mat. Hauling the extremely hot tray to the chair circle took skill and even more luck. The volunteer cooks offered to move it, but the crew knew better than to let them try. If a couple of the chicken breasts ended up in the sand, God only knew what would happen to the hot coals.

Andrew pulled a couple of large pieces of firewood off his raft and set them on the coals. It didn't take long before the flames from the fire lit the rock wall behind us. Even though there were enough O.A.R.S. canvas chairs for all of the passengers and crew, Andy always brought his special chair to the circle. It was a simple wooden chair that broke down into two pieces so it could be stored flat in his dory. Turquoise colored paint once covered the the wood, but much of the color had worn off. The canvas back had a patch sewn on that read "Banjos Not Bombs."

That night, as we were all starting to wind down, Andy pulled his chair close to the fire and then walked away. He disappeared into the darkness by the water. A few minutes later he returned with a guitar case and a banjo case.

Andy played an eclectic list of songs, mostly folksy tunes. We sang along to a few of them. One was titled *Let him go on, Mama*, which I'd never heard before. It has a couple of lines in its refrain that are a boatmen favorite: "Well it's too thick to navigate, and it's too thin to plow." The song is referring to a river, presumably the Mississippi. Andy smiled every time he sang those lines.

He took a break from playing to switch instruments. I mistakenly thought he was finished. I asked, "You're not calling it a night, are you?"

"No. But I was thinking about getting a beer."

"You play, I'll get you a beer."

"Well, alright. I'll keep playing as long as you're buying."

I went to JB's raft and brought a beer back for Andy. "Here you go. It's the least I can do to thank you for the music."

He opened it, took a sip, and said to me, "Thank you for the beer, Matt."

"You're welcome," I said. "It's Phill's."

Most of the crew had already gone to sleep by the time Andy started his second set. Several were snoozing no more than thirty feet from where he sat and played. The music outlasted me as well. Karen and I slipped away from the group and got ready for bed. It was probably the combination of us being exhausted, the peaceful setting, and the brilliant stars that eased our fears about things messing with us in the middle of the night. We did make sure to check our sleeping bags for uninvited guests before we crawled into them.

Lying there, we appreciated how fortunate we were, not just for having the opportunity to take the trip, but also for the company of our fellow passengers, the all-star crew, the weather, and now, the incredible night sky. Karen had said many times before that she would like to fall asleep looking at the stars. This was her chance. The light from the fire was making it a little difficult to see the Milky Way, but before we dozed off the fire was out. That night I fell asleep while searching for shooting stars.

The guys grilling chicken by headlamp.

Andy playing guitar at night by the fire.

DAY THREE

I didn't wake up in the middle of the night, which is rare for me. Blinking my eyes open I could see Karen peacefully sleeping in her bag. The night passed without incident: no snakes, no rodents, no stinging critters of any kind had bothered us. Nothing sniffed us or crawled into our sleeping bags, at least as far as we knew.

None of the other passengers were up when the crew blew the conch shell. I stumbled down the sand embankment to fill my O.A.R.S. cup with coffee. Maia was sitting on the sleep pad on top of her raft, playing her saxophone. I wondered where she stowed it during the day to keep it from getting soaked. Betsy and JB were bustling around the food prep area. There was a large bowl of pancake batter sitting on one of the stainless steel tables ready for the grill.

Later, when most of the passengers were sitting in the chair circle eating breakfast, I mentioned how well I'd slept. Lolly replied, "I didn't sleep a wink last night!"

"What kept you up?" I asked.

"We were right next to the latrine."

"Did the smell bother you?"

"No, it wasn't the smell. People kept walking past us all night going to the bathroom. It was Grand Central Station over there."

"OK, good to know; don't sleep by the toilet area. Why were you over there in the first place?"

"I wanted to be close to the latrine in case I had to go in the middle of the night. I think after last night I'd rather use a blue bucket."

Craig said, "I slept like a baby, but I kept having this dream that Aya was trying to hold my hand in the middle of the night. I was half asleep when it occurred to me that Aya was on my right side, and I was feeling something touch my left hand. I looked down and saw a ringtail cat sniffing me."

Karen gasped.

"Craig, Craig, Craig," I said shaking my head, "Maybe we should save the critter stories for when we're in the bar at the El Tovar."

"He was cute," Craig said. "I shook my hand and he scurried off. I'm sure the same one visited you guys last night. You just didn't know it."

Karen grabbed my arm. I said to her, "It's a cat. You like cats. And if there's a cat around, there won't be any mice."

"I'm going to act like I didn't hear any of this," she said, and went to refill her coffee.

Being our second morning waking up on the river, we were beginning to acclimate to river time. My first instinct would be to grab a quick breakfast, pack and get on the river. But things move slower in the canyon. Granted, all I had to do was take care of myself and my stuff; the crew had to make breakfast, clean up afterward, and load all of the gear. Even with the passengers helping, it takes a while to be ready to shove off in the morning. I had plenty of time to practice properly sealing my dry bag so as not to have a repeat of yesterday's leakage.

We paired with John and Lolly again for the day. We later learned that the other passengers were frowning on us for doing so. They were switching each day so they could ride with a different couple. To be clear, the other couples were switching not swapping.

As the four of us were standing on the beach with our life

jackets on, Karen said, "It looks like all of the other couples are swapping, maybe we should too."

John replied, "Nice. What happens in the Grand Canyon, stays in the Grand Canyon."

I added, "It's a little early in the day to be suggesting something like that, don't you think?"

"Are you guys twelve years old? You know what I mean," Karen said.

"Then you shouldn't have used the word 'swap,' " I said.

"I thought I was talking to adults. There's nothing wrong with using the word 'swap.' "

"OK, then go over there and ask Phill if he'd like to swap with us and see what he says. Brush your hair back and tilt your head slightly when you ask him, maybe put your hand on his shoulder. Just don't say that I think it's a good idea too."

"You *are* twelve."

"Go ahead and ask him. We'll wait here and watch."

Karen didn't offer to swap with anyone. Or if she did, she didn't tell me about it. Lolly wasn't interested in switching couples, "No, let's stay together for the entire trip. Everyone else can switch or swap or whatever they're doing."

I disagreed, "We need to be more sociable. Tomorrow we should pair up with different couples. And Karen can swap if she wants."

When it was time to Dories, Ho!, we asked Eric if we could ride in his dory, the *Marble Canyon*. We didn't need rain gear or helmets. In contrast to the day before when we went through a slew of rapids, today there would only be a few small rapids. All that flat water made for a peaceful day on the river, but a lot of rowing for the boatmen.

Our first stop was six miles down the river: the proposed site for the Marble Canyon Dam at mile 40. Other than 36-Mile Rapid and a few unnamed rapids and riffles, the river was calm on our way to the site. As we made our way, Eric told us about the attempts by the Bureau of Reclamation to build Marble Canyon Dam and Martin Litton's campaign to prevent it.

The Colorado River hasn't been a wild river in Arizona for nearly a century. In the far western part of the state, on the Nevada-Arizona border, the Hoover Dam (completed in 1936) blocks the river, forming Lake Mead behind it. In the east, at Page, Arizona, the Glen Canyon Dam (completed in 1963) also blocks the river and forms Lake Powell behind it. Both dams were built to generate electricity, control flooding, and to manage the distribution of water to cities and farms in the Southwest.

The Federal Government built Hoover Dam during the Great Depression. It faced opposition from environmentalists, but at the time, the economic benefits overshadowed the environmental risks. The construction of the Glen Canyon Dam faced much more opposition. Not only was it built during a time of greater economic prosperity, its location was also of grave concern to outdoor enthusiasts. In 1963, when its gates were closed, Glen Canyon Dam began to flood a sublime canyon behind it, a canyon with irreplaceable beauty and human history. It took seventeen years for Lake Powell to fill completely, but prior to that, in 1972, the Glen Canyon National Recreation Area was established as a unit of the National Park Service to provide the public recreational access to the lake.

In addition to Glen Canyon Dam and Hoover Dam, the U.S. Bureau of Reclamation had proposed additional dams along the Colorado River. Two of them would have had profound impacts on the Grand Canyon. Bridge Canyon Dam, 235 miles downstream of Lees Ferry, would have stood 740 feet tall: fourteen feet taller than Hoover Dam. The reservoir behind it would have extended well into the park.

Marble Canyon Dam would have been constructed about forty river miles below Lees Ferry. Its reservoir would have flooded much of the canyon we'd floated through during the previous two days, including Redwall Cavern. The two dams would have created a funding source for other Bureau projects through the sale of the electricity they would produce. These projects would be the "cash register"—the words the Bureau used—for future projects.

To rally support for the Marble Canyon Dam, the Bureau insisted that the area between Lees Ferry and the mouth of the Little Colorado River wasn't the Grand Canyon at all, rather they argued that it was a separate canyon, Marble Canyon. They figured it would be easier to garner support if the public thought the flooded area wasn't part of the Grand Canyon.

One of Martin Litton's laments toward the end of his life was that he didn't do enough to prevent the construction of Glen Canyon Dam. Whether he could have succeeded in stopping its construction we'll never know, but he did play a central role in motivating people to speak out against Marble Canyon Dam. He put up a fierce fight, primarily by encouraging the Sierra Club and its members to protest the building of the dam.

People kept telling him he should be reasonable and compromise. He wouldn't have it. In a 1994 interview with *boatman's quarterly review* he said, "When you compromise nature, nature gets compromised." In 1968, the Bureau abandoned their plans to build Marble Canyon Dam.

Litton had good reason to be leery of compromise. It was a compromise that led to the construction of Glen Canyon Dam. At the time it was proposing the Glen Canyon Dam, the Bureau was also proposing to build a dam on the Colorado River in what is today Dinosaur National Monument. Eventually, the Sierra Club and others agreed to not oppose the Glen Canyon Dam project if the Bureau agreed to scrap their plans to build the dam in Dinosaur National Monument. To Litton, this was unacceptable, and going forward he wouldn't back down from the causes he believed in.

Prior to killing the project, the Bureau conducted tests at the proposed Marble Canyon Dam site. This included setting off dynamite at strategic locations to determine the integrity of the rock. At the spot on the river where the Bureau had done their tests, the boatmen pulled their dories and rafts close to each other, forming a flotilla. We all held onto the boat next us to keep from drifting apart. Andre stood, and with a cautionary tone gave us a history lesson about the threats to the canyon and what might have been if not for people like Litton.

Looking up at the canyon walls where the dam would have stood, we could imagine the scenery we'd seen in the previous forty miles buried beneath a reservoir, with jet skis careening across the top of it. The message Andre and the other boatmen were trying to deliver is that, before he died, Martin Litton passed the torch to us and future generations to be stewards of these incredible places. The Grand Canyon belongs to us all, and we must protect it.

The next four miles of the river were flat and calm. At one point the river flowed directly east for a mile or so, and then made a 180-degree turn and headed back to the west. At the apex of the turn, we ran President Harding Rapid, the roughest water we experienced that day, but still a relatively small rapid. The curve in the river formed a gooseneck, a piece of land in the shape of the neck of a goose, looming high above us: Point Hansbrough.

We made a quick stop for lunch and then continued downstream. There were areas where the river was so calm that the surrounding canyon walls were reflected as mirror images on the water. I kept taking pictures of the view with my phone and then looking at them on the screen. I realized after a few attempts that there was no way to capture the splendor of the place in a photo, let alone a snapshot on my phone. I put my phone back in my dry bag, sat back and just absorbed the scenery.

Karen always says at times like this, "Soak it in. We don't get these days back." She's right. Whenever we travel, we are keenly aware of how finite our time is. Not in a worrisome way, but we have a healthy respect for the possibility that whatever we are doing at that moment might be the last or only time we do it. I enjoy having photos of places we've been, but not at the expense of missing out on the experience because I was too busy taking pictures.

At mile 47, Eric asked, "Are you guys up for a hike?"

"We're always up for a hike," I replied.

"I think we'll pull over here and stretch our legs then."

Eric pulled the *Marble Canyon* onto a wide beach. The other boats, like ducklings following mama, did the same. "I've been looking forward to this hike ever since the side canyon flooded last month," Eric said. He was talking about Saddle Canyon. The hike to its pour-off has been a favorite of boatmen and river trippers for decades. Heavy rains in August caused a flood that scoured the canyon below the pour-off. The flood was powerful enough to wash rock debris into the main channel of the Colorado River.

As was the case the day before, all of the passengers and crew went on the hike. It didn't take long to get to our destination, which was about a mile from the river. Even at a leisurely pace, we arrived in about forty-five minutes. Eric was leading the hike and stopped just short of the end of the canyon. I was at the back of the line so I couldn't hear what he was saying to the others who were standing with him, but I could see him pointing to a spot on the sidewall about ten feet above his head. Then, he looked back toward the river and held his hands above his head in disbelief.

"What's up?" I asked when I caught up with the group.

"We're wondering what happened to the boulder," Rondo said.

"What boulder?" I asked.

"Exactly," he replied.

The boatmen said that for as long as they can remember hiking up this canyon, there had been a boulder at the spot where we were standing. They called it a chokestone: a rock that makes it difficult or impossible for hikers to get past it in a slot canyon. One of the challenges of this hike used to be getting everyone up and over the chokestone so they could make it to the end of the canyon. When we got home from the trip, I searched online for pictures of this spot in hopes of getting a look at the boulder. I found photos of several hikers standing on top of it. One blogger estimated that it weighed about fifty tons. That's a big rock, and it was nowhere to be found. The flood had not only dislodged the boulder, but the waters carried it away. Maybe the stone was now sitting at the bottom of the Colorado River, or maybe it was pulverized into countless pieces. Whatever happened, it was no longer blocking the trail.

"I kind of feel like we're cheating now," said Andy. He reached down and felt the underside of the canyon wall about knee high. "We had to grab right here and pull up. See this handhold? That used to be above my head." The same flood that obliterated the chokestone must have deposited the sand we were standing on. The floor of the canyon was now several feet higher than it was the last time any of the boatmen had been here.

Several yards past where the boulder had been was a trickle of a waterfall about thirty feet high. Some of the boatmen and crew stood under the pour-off like it was a shower. Each couple took a turn having their picture taken with the pour-off in the background; then we had one of the crew take a group photo of all the passengers. It was cool back in the shade of the canyon, and we all hung out there and rested. It was a nice break from the heat of the mid-day sun.

We spent the rest of the afternoon floating on mirror-calm waters. Karen sat in the back of the dory with her arms folded across her chest, taking in the sublime scenery. Around every turn of the river was another postcard worthy vista. The civilized world seemed a million miles away. It made me wonder what would happen if someone needed to get in touch with us while we were on the river.

Eric had a satellite phone with him that he could use to call the O.A.R.S. office if needed. He could contact them, but they couldn't contact him. We found out when we reached

Phantom Ranch that Eric hadn't called the office since we left Lees Ferry. I liked the fact that we were out of touch with the rest of the world. Whatever news had to be found out, or whatever message had to be conveyed, could wait. That's a rare thing these days.

Hanging out at the Saddle Canyon pour-off.

The *Marble Canyon* dory.

JB rowing a raft while Q supervises from the back.

NANKOWEAP CAMP

Our camp for the night was the Main Nankoweap camp on the west side of the river. On our approach to the site, we saw hikers coming down a trail from the west. Eric said they were hiking on the Nankoweap Trail, which runs from the north rim of the canyon to the river.

Once we floated through Nankoweap Rapid and beached the boats at our campsite, we never saw the hikers again. It's possible they camped close to the river just north of us on the delta formed by Nankoweap Creek entering the Colorado River. Karen was already making plans in her head for us to do the hike next year, but her subsequent research, once we got home, put an end to that idea.

A National Park Service trail description notes: *"This trail is classified as MOST difficult of the named trails in Grand Canyon."* I've read that the trailhead on the north rim is hard to get to and even harder to find. And there is almost no water on the trail, which means hikers have to carry all the water they'll need with them. The National Park Service also advises that hikers cache water along the trail for their return trip.

What makes the Nankoweap Trail most difficult though, are the sections that are precariously narrow with steep drop-offs. It's not a hike for the faint of heart. Long before the area was made a National Park, legend has it that horse thieves used the trail to avoid capture. They would steal horses in Utah, bring them down to the river along the Nankoweap Trail, cross the river and lead them out of the canyon on the Tanner Trail. Once out of the canyon, they would sell the horses further south in Arizona. After unloading their stolen horses, the thieves would repeat the process, but this time stealing in Arizona and selling in Utah. That's a tough way to make a living.

There are other trails from the North and South Rims to the river. Some of them are not considered trails so much as merely paths or routes. To help visitors from making bad or possibly fatal decisions, the National Park Service has classified all of the trails in the park into one of four zones.

The **Corridor Zone** includes the popular trails that most of us are familiar with, like Bright Angel, South Kaibab, and North Kaibab. These are suitable for hikers without previous experience in the Grand Canyon, and provide conveniences like drinking water along the trails, paved roads to trailheads, toilets, signs and ranger stations. There are even benches to nap on.

The next level of difficulty is the **Threshold Zone**, recommended for hikers with experience in the Grand Canyon. Trails in this zone are not maintained and have scarce water sources and dirt roads to trail heads.

More difficult still is the **Primitive Zone**, recommended for highly experienced hikers with proven route-finding ability. The trails in this zone are not maintained trails, require a four-wheel-drive vehicle to reach the trailheads, and have limited signage. Both the Tanner and Nankoweap Trails are in the Primitive Zone.

The most difficult zone is the **Wild Zone**, recommended only for highly experienced hikers with extensive route-finding ability. And possibly a death wish. There aren't defined trails in the Wild Zone, but rather indistinct or non-existent routes, mostly vertical, with water sources scarce to non-existent.

We'll probably never venture out of the Corridor Zone,

but the benefit of having Karen research these trails is that now when I mention that we still need to hike the fourteen-mile North Kaibab Trail, it seems like a piece of cake to her.

We were now approaching our third evening. Looking back, I'm surprised at how quickly we adapted to life on the river. When we arrived at our campsite each evening, we would help unload the boats, set up our sleeping area, explore the landscape around our new campsite, and meet at the support rafts for a beer. Everyone had enough time to be alone and to be with the group. There was nothing to think about other than what you were doing that very moment.

The Nankoweap campsite was flat and had lots of room for each couple to find a private spot. The large crescent-shaped beach blocked our view of the campsite to the south where another group was staying. We were settling into our river routine: laying out our blue tarps and sleeping bags, and arranging all the stuff we would need once the sun went down so we could find it all. A few in our group braved the cold and bathed in the river at the far end of the beach. Karen and I preferred using the adult wipes rather than risking heart failure in the river.

That night I forgot to bring my headlamp to dinner. I realized this in plenty of time to go back and get it while there was still light in the sky, but I didn't. I got caught up in more interesting activities like a conversation with the other passengers and having seconds of chocolate cake. I waited until way past dark before I decided to go to our sleeping area to get it. "How hard could it be to find our spot?" I thought to myself. We'd set up about a hundred and fifty feet away from the chair circle, and there was a path through the brush to our sleeping area.

I got lost. And not kind of lost, but "Crap! I'm lost!" lost. There was never a time I couldn't see a light: either the solar lights from the kitchen area or another person's headlamp. But whenever I tried to get back to where I thought the chair circle was, I would run into what seemed to be an impenetrable wall of scrub. At first, not knowing how to get back was merely an annoyance. Then it turned into a mild panic. Finally, I'd been gone long enough that I thought Karen might be worrying about me. I no longer cared if there were snakes or thorns or ring-tailed whatevers in the bushes. I pushed my way through every thicket between me and what I could see as the circle of headlamps in the chair circle.

When I emerged from the bush, wild-eyed and bleeding from scrapes on both arms and both legs, I expected the group to be relieved to see me. No one even looked up. That's not true. Phill looked at me and said, "Hey, Matt. If you're going to the rafts for a beer, I'll have another." I took a deep breath, ignored him and found Karen. I sat down next to her and asked to borrow her headlamp so I could find my way to our sleeping area to get mine. She said, "Sure. What happened there? It looks like you're bleeding?"

"I tried to go get my headlamp in the dark and got lost. I had to climb through some scrub to get back."

"You got lost? Our sleeping bags are right over there. How could you get lost?" As she said this, she shook her head and pointed into the dark as if scolding a child. Let me just say for the record that the direction she was pointing was *not* the direction of our sleeping area. But I was in no position to argue, so I took her headlamp and re-started my odyssey.

Not soon after my adventure in the dark, Karen and I decided to call it a night. It was the first night that we had a 360-degree view of the stars. The night before, the sky was clear, yet we were sleeping next to a cliff that blocked about half of our view of the sky. The Milky Way was as clear that night as I've ever seen it. Karen has a thing for the Milky Way, who doesn't really? Once you've seen it, you can't help but be fascinated by it.

Lying there looking up, I was struck by how much movement there was in the sky. Some of the specks of light were moving. They looked too high to be airplanes; maybe they were satellites. Occasionally, we saw shooting stars.

Some were short, tiny streaks. Others shot in long bright arcs across the sky. Searching for shooting stars becomes addictive; it's impossible not to look for the next one. The next thing I remember was hearing the sound of the conch shell.

Dories and rafts beached for the evening.

DAY FOUR

There's not much to do at 6:00 am except pee and check my belongings to make sure nothing was carried off in the night. I could see someone stirring about the kitchen area. In the first light of the day, I was a little embarrassed to notice how few bushes there were in the area. Even on a random walk through camp, I don't think I could have run into as much vegetation as I had the night before. It's a good thing I hadn't startled a rattlesnake, although maybe I did without knowing it. The snake would have certainly thought, "This guy is too stupid to bite. I'm going to move to another bush and stay out of his way."

The plan for the day was to do a hike before we continued down the river. We had a long, relaxing morning; it was sunny, yet the temperature was comfortable. After breakfast, the crew broke down camp and loaded the boats, so that when we got back from the hike, there would be very little to do except to shove off.

About a mile behind our campsite, a rock wall rose high above the river. At the base of the cliff, stretching a half of a mile or so toward the river was a fan of rock debris. The rock running up to the vertical cliff was a gray/greenish color. Much of the green color was from vegetation that was still colorful from the rains a few days earlier. Where the rock became vertical, its color was distinctively red.

The day before, as we were approaching the shore, Eric had directed our attention to the cliff. At the bottom of the vertical section, about 700 feet above the river, were several rectangle-shaped openings. If he hadn't pointed them out, we probably would never have seen the ancient Puebloan granaries nestled in the cliff. They looked tiny from the river. Those granaries were the destination of our morning hike.

All of the passengers and crew went on the hike, although a few who were skittish about heights considered staying behind. But the enticement of seeing the pristine ruins up close was enough for them to set aside their fears and brave the trail. It's a fairly steep, 700 foot scramble to the cliffs where the granaries are, which makes you wonder why the Puebloans stored their grain in such an inaccessible place.

Eric led the hike, and we were a little confused when he started out by taking us in a direction upriver, away from the granaries. We'd been hiking for about a quarter of a mile when he stopped at a small rise that overlooked the river. Eric was standing on the flat top of a low hill, a few remaining sections of a rock wall surrounded the area. Once the entire group reached the spot where Eric had stopped, he explained the significance of where we were standing.

He said, "Do you see this here?" as he pointed to a broad flat rock that had a concave top surface. Sitting on top of the flat rock was a smaller, round stone about twice the size of my hand. "This is a fine example of a mano and metate. This area where we are standing is where the Puebloans lived. We think they lived here about 800 to 1,000 years ago. They used these stones to grind their grain into flour."

"If they lived down here, why did they put the granaries way up there?" one of the passengers asked.

"Not sure. Why do you think they put them up there?" Eric responded.

"Maybe to protect their food from flood waters, or insects?" suggested Paul.

I said, "I don't know, but they must not have intended to

use them on a daily basis. I doubt I'd be hiking up there every time Karen needed corn to make a batch of tortillas." It was a mile trek to reach them from where we were standing.

Karen said, "You mean if I were down here making the meals and taking care of the children—keeping the wild animals from snatching them—you wouldn't run up there for me?"

"Maybe once. The second time, I probably wouldn't come back."

"As long as there's food involved, I think you'd keep coming back," she said.

It was hard for me to imagine raising a family in a place this remote a thousand years ago. Karen and I have raised children of our own, and we know how much work and attention it takes to keep a toddler alive in a modern home. I can't imagine how difficult it must have been to survive in the wilderness with no support from the outside world and a swift-flowing river in your front yard.

The hike up to the granaries took about thirty minutes. It was moderately strenuous, and there were times the footing was a little tricky when we had to climb over rocks. It was a good thing we were doing the hike before the day got too warm. In full sun and the middle of the day, it would have been a brutal hike.

For most of the way, the trail was wide enough that we didn't worry about steep drop-offs. But right before reaching the granaries, there were a couple of short sections of the trail where we had to be careful where we placed our feet to avoid falling. Everyone was paying close attention to each other and making sure there were no traffic jams at those precarious spots, so each person had plenty of time and space to make it through without incident.

I was surprised at how small the inside of the granaries were. The Puebloans had built them into the side of a natural overhang of the cliff by stacking rocks from floor to ceiling and leaving a small opening at the front. Sitting ten feet away from the granaries, it made more sense why they were so hard to see from the river. When we were there, all of the openings were uncovered. Most likely when the Indians who built these nooks used them, they would have concealed the openings with rocks. This would have kept animals out and made them even harder to see from a distance.

Our group sat on the ledges just beneath the openings and took a twenty-minute break. From our sunny vantage point, we had an unobstructed view downstream of three miles of the river. The sun reflected off the water making the river look like a silver streak. It was a magnificent sight, one we could have sat and gazed at for much longer, but we had a lot to do that day so we got moving again.

At the river, we broke our routine of riding with John and Lolly and paired with Phill and Wendy for the day. We rode with Andre in his dory, the *Black Canyon*. From Nankoweap we traveled nine miles down the river to the confluence of the Little Colorado and Colorado Rivers. The confluence is the point where the Bureau of Reclamation claimed that Marble Canyon ends and the Grand Canyon begins. Martin Litton was adamant that the Grand Canyon began at Lees Ferry. We beached our boats just shy of the mouth of the Little Colorado. Eric had on our itinerary a mid-day break to walk up the Little Colorado a mile or so.

The boatmen had a hard time finding a place to pull up to shore where we could get out of the dories without sinking mid-shin deep in mud. The shallow, grassy shoreline caught the silt that was generated by the storms a few days earlier. We had to bushwhack our way through tall vegetation to find the narrow path that ran parallel to the river. Once we made it through a couple of hundred feet of thick undergrowth, the trail became dry. From there, the rest of the walk was on flat, hard rock—almost like a sidewalk.

The Little Colorado River runs through the Navajo Indian Reservation, but the Navajo and the U.S. Government dispute the exact boundary where Navajo land ends and the national park begins. In a nutshell, the Navajo claim that the center of the river is the boundary; the U.S. Government asserts that the high-water level on the east bank of the river is the boundary. Their dispute may seem unimportant, but it's not. The Navajo have contemplated developing a tourist destination on the east bank of the Colorado River at the mouth of the Little Colorado. Doing so would only be legal if the land on the bank of the river is theirs.

Several times during our hike along the river we stopped and Eric told us interesting historical facts about the area. At one of the stops, we could see the remnants of a stone cabin on the south side of the river that a prospector named Ben Beamer built in 1890. Beamer tucked the cabin underneath an overhanging cliff so that the cliff formed the back wall and ceiling. He also incorporated part of an ancient Puebloan ruin into the structure. Beamer was living in the area to search for gold and silver. Like many prospectors in the Grand Canyon, he found more copper and asbestos than gold and silver.

It was probably Powell's stories about the canyon that drew Beamer's attention to the area. Two short decades before Beamer built his cabin, Powell and his crew became the first westerners to navigate the length of the Colorado River through the Grand Canyon.

Reports of Powell's successful trip drew attention to the area and made him somewhat of a celebrity. His accomplishment was remarkable enough on its own merit, but even more so when considering that Powell had lost his right arm below the elbow in a Civil War battle years before the river expedition. Powell repeated the route down the river two years later when he was able to document and survey the canyon more accurately.

In a relatively short period of time afterward, the canyon saw significant development. Seventeen years after Powell's first expedition, 1.8 million acres of the surrounding landscape was designated a forest reserve. In 1903, the El Tovar Hotel was completed on the South Rim, in 1908 Theodore Roosevelt made the area a National Monument, and in 1919 Congress made it a National Park.

According to river historian, Otis Reed "Dock" Marston,

counting Powell and crew, the 100th person to float the length of the canyon did so in 1950. The National Park Service estimates that today over 20,000 people each year take a trip down the Colorado River through the Grand Canyon during the seven to eight month season.

Just like the Colorado River, the waters of the Little Colorado were still murky from runoff caused by the rains. Passengers on a Colorado River trip often swim or float down the Little Colorado River while wearing life vests. They turn the life jackets upside down, put their legs through the armholes, and cinch it tight. The life jacket keeps them above water and cushions their bottoms in case they bump into rocks in the shallow areas.

Before our trip, I'd seen photos of people making a human chain—like a sit-down conga line—and floating through the turquoise-colored water. The natural blue color comes from calcium carbonate in the water, similar to the blue water we'd seen in Havasu Creek. On this trip, however, the water wasn't turquoise; it was brown. And none of us were tempted to get into the muddy water.

When we shoved off, our "Dories, Ho!" was so weak Rondo made us do it again. It was late in the day, and the group's energy level was low. If I were home, it would be naptime. But I wasn't home. I was on an amazing trip in the middle of the Grand Canyon, so I needed to rally.

Soon after we got back onto the river, we ran through a set of riffles that took us past a delta island that sits right where the Little Colorado dumps into the Colorado River. The island would make a nice campsite, but the National Park Service prohibits camping there. We had a few more miles to go to get to our campsite for the night.

View from the trail to the granaries. The granaries are in the depression in the cliff to the right, the Colorado River to the left.

Left to right: Bart, Joe and Q. Looking through JB's book
The Hidden Canyon: A River Journey.

CRASH CANYON

As we floated peacefully, we could hear conversation in the boats behind us. A boatman in one of the other dories said, "I've heard people say that if the angle of the sun is just right, you can see where the propeller left spiral marks on the side of the cliff." We were at mile 63, and everyone was looking up at Chuar and Temple Buttes west of the river.

"What the heck are they talking about?" I asked Andre.

"This is the site of the plane crash."

"Plane crash?" I asked.

"Years ago two airliners collided over the Grand Canyon, and this is where it happened."

Having been in a mid-air plane collision while in Alaska several years before, we have a keen interest in aviation disasters. I turned to Karen—she being my research assistant whose job it is to know everything about everything—and asked, "Did you know this?"

"Never heard of it."

Wow! How could it be that we hadn't heard about this before now? Granted, it happened a few years before we were born. When we returned home, we read everything we could find about the crash. It's a fascinating and tragic story.

On June 30, 1956, two passenger planes collided 21,000 feet above the canyon. It was a Saturday. One of the planes was a United Airlines DC-7. At the time, DC-7's were the newest, fastest planes in United's fleet. The United flight had fifty-eight people on board. The other plane was a TWA Super Constellation with seventy on board. The crash killed all 128 passengers and crew.

Both planes took off from Los Angeles within a few minutes of each other. One headed for Chicago, the other for Kansas City. They were supposed to be on different flight paths and flying at different altitudes, but a series of events caused them to be in the exact same place at the exact same time, over the Grand Canyon. No one knows the precise details of what brought the planes together. The United flight was flying at its assigned altitude of 21,000 feet. The TWA flight initially flew at its assigned altitude of 19,000 feet, but once in the air requested an altitude of 21,000 feet due to weather. Air Traffic Control denied TWA's request for 21,000 feet, yet later approved a second request by the TWA pilots to fly 1,000 feet above the clouds. The TWA flight then climbed to 21,000 feet, which put it on a collision course with the United flight. Back then, flying above the clouds in this manner was allowed so long as the pilots followed visual flight rules, which essentially meant "don't hit another plane."

If this all sounds confusing, it's because it *is* confusing. One of the conclusions of the investigation was that neither pilot was clearly to blame for the accident. Rather, the rules at the time were such that even if both pilots obeyed the rules, their planes could still collide.

The report from the investigation stated that the two planes might not have seen each other until the very last moment before impact. There were storm clouds in the area at the time of the crash and investigators speculate that both planes could have been maneuvering around the same cloud from opposite directions, thus not able to see each other until it was too late.

I've seen the Grand Canyon from the air when flying on commercial flights between Seattle and Phoenix. The view is spectacular on a clear day. It's possible that the pilots of the doomed aircraft were angling for a better view of the canyon for their passengers, which put them on a collision course. In 1956, maneuvering to provide passengers a prime view of the canyon wasn't uncommon and not considered dangerous, again, so long as the pilots obeyed visual flight rules.

Investigators believe that the United plane struck the TWA plane from behind and at an angle causing the TWA plane's tail to detach and the fuselage to decompress rapidly. They came to this conclusion partly because searchers found light debris strewn across a wide area below the site of the collision, which would have been the result of the plane spewing debris from inside the fuselage while it was still in the air. They also found the tail of the TWA plane more than 500 yards away from the rest of the wreckage and a piece of the United plane's left wing close to the TWA tail.

The collision caused the TWA plane to go into a near vertical dive. It crashed into a ravine somewhere on the north side of Temple Butte. The United plane most likely lost nearly all of its control and went into a downward, left turn. It struck the south face of Chuar Butte over 600 feet above the river.

The scene must have been horrific, but no one saw it until hours later. In 1956, there were very few people on the river. It wasn't until late in the day that two brothers, who operated a small air taxi service in the Grand Canyon, spotted the wreckage from the air.

In 2014, the crash site was designated a National Historic Landmark. In the spring of 2017, Karen and I visited the Desert Tower area on the South Rim of the Grand Canyon, where the National Park Service has placed a commemorative plaque by the rim of the canyon. The day we were there, crowds of people swarmed the area around Desert Tower. Visitors lined the fences along the rim that protect them from going over the edge. On a cloudless day, like it was when we were there, a person looking in the direction of the accident site would have easily seen two planes crashing into the canyon. It's possible that no one standing there would have seen the initial mid-air collision, but they would have seen smoke rising from the canyon immediately afterward. It's remarkable that there were no credible eyewitnesses to the event. The fact that no one witnessed the accident and it took a few hours to report the smoke is another indication of how much smaller the crowds must have been in the 1950s.

When it happened, the 1956 Grand Canyon mid-air collision was the deadliest U.S. commercial airline disaster ever. The press extensively covered the event and the investigation that followed. Even though more deadly airline disasters have occurred since, many believe that the 1956 disaster was the main catalyst for dramatic improvements to the Air Traffic Control system, the formation of the Federal Aviation Administration (FAA), and eventually the requirement that all commercial flights carry flight recorders (black boxes). Neither of the planes involved in the crash had black boxes aboard.

Floating past the area, I would never have guessed that two planes crashed there. And it's possible that the wreckage wouldn't have been visible from the river on the day of the accident. To the extent they could, investigators and the National Park Service have kept the exact location of the crash sites hidden from the public record. There are stories of people visiting the area to look for pieces of wreckage or debris. The National Park Service not only discourages this, but they also closed the area to the public in the late 1950s. It remains closed today.

CARBON CAMP

Somewhere between mile 63 and Carbon Camp at mile 65, we stopped to bathe. I overheard one of the boatmen say to a passenger earlier in the day something to the effect of, "Typically the day we visit the Little Colorado is a good day to stop and bathe in the river. There is a spot where a side creek enters the river, and the water is shallow by the shore. We can't bathe in the side creek, but on a sunny day like today, the water in the shallow areas of the river is usually warmer than in the main channel."

As we landed the boats on a low beach, the other passengers were excited about the prospect of bathing. I didn't see a side creek, but there was, however, a sandbar that hooked into the river and formed a shallow, protected cove along the shore. We hadn't been out of the dories but a few minutes when most of the passengers headed toward the cove with their camp suds. Ever since the start of the trip when I saw how muddy the river was and felt the frigid temperature of the water, I was dubious of taking a bath, but the group hysteria sucked me in. At least, I thought, it would be an opportunity to soap and rinse the clothes I was wearing at the time; I wasn't about to strip down and go under.

I got my camp soap out of my dry bag; I'd put it there before we loaded the boats that morning when I heard we'd be stopping at a warm spot to bathe. Carefully, I waded in up to my waist. The water was frigid. It couldn't have been a single degree warmer than the main channel of the river. But I was already half in, so I took off my shirt, soaped it and began rinsing it off. Then I did something stupid. Without thinking it through, I decided to wash my hair as long as I was already in the river. I quickly lathered my head and then realized there was no way to rinse it off without going all of the way under water. I had wanted to avoid this; I tend to panic in cold water.

My fellow passengers had a grand time watching me and laughing as I tried to put just my head in the water. I could see Karen standing on the beach—safely dry I might add—looking at me and shaking her head. She wasn't laughing. She had an expression of pity on her face. It was saying, "Have you lost your mind? You're like a dog trying to get a protective cone off its head after visiting the vet. Man up and go under!" Finally, I took the plunge. I'm sure my heart stopped for at least a few beats. When I came up, there was still soap all over my head, so I had to go under a couple of more times. "Wow!" I thought, "That was *not* worth it. Now I feel gritty all over."

Karen never got into the water; she was too busy taking pictures. She may have been the only passenger who didn't go in. Even John, with all of his protesting and bluster prior to the trip, lathered up and went under. Now that I think about it, I don't recall any of the boatmen or crew getting in either. I remember them standing on the shore and looking at us like we were idiots. Truth be told, even if you come out of the river a little bit cleaner than you went in, you don't stay clean very long. Within a couple of hours, you'll be back to being filthy again. The crew knew that once you've built up a layer of dirt and funk on your body, you should just leave it be, it's part of the experience.

Later that night I looked on Karen's phone at the photos of the group bathing. I kept scrolling through them trying to figure out who was who; everyone looked different with fewer clothes on. I asked Karen, "Who is the fat, white, walrus-looking guy in this picture?"

"Let me see," she said. "I don't know who you're talking about."

"Right there. That bald guy with his back to the camera who looks like his upper body hasn't seen the sun in the last decade? Wait! Crap! That's me isn't it?"

"I think you look hot," she replied.

I raised my hand and asked, "How many fingers am I holding up?"

I learned a lot that afternoon: don't bathe in a cold, muddy river, don't ever again take my shirt off in public, and Karen is legally blind.

That evening we camped at mile 65, just past where Carbon Creek enters the Colorado River. It was the largest campsite we'd stayed at so far. There was a bit of an elevation gain a hundred yards or so back from the river where we set up our sleeping area. We were just high enough to have a sweeping view of the campsite and river.

Karen and I claimed a spot in front of several large boulders, which formed a natural screen from the rest of the site. On nights we didn't put up our tent, Karen had to wait until dark to change her clothes. With the rocks there, she was able to change behind them in relaxed privacy. It's interesting how quickly small things like a little privacy become a luxury on a trip like this.

It was our fourth night, and I was surprised at how much Karen was enjoying the experience of living on the river. It's not that I thought she wouldn't enjoy it, but for some people, sleeping on the ground, living out of a dry bag and brushing their teeth in the river can get old quickly. I'd thought that might be the case with Karen. It wasn't. She loved every minute of the trip. I was beginning to be hopeful that she might even want to do more sleeping outside in the future. Time will tell.

Our evening routine that night was similar to the nights before: dinner was great, and we sat around the chair circle laughing about the events of the day, especially bathing in the frigid river. As soon as the sun went down, I couldn't keep my eyes open. Karen and I got ready for bed early and laid in our sleeping bags looking at the night sky. The stars were brighter that night than any of the other nights on the trip.

Then I heard her giggle.

"What's so funny?" I asked.

"I just had a flashback."

"You mean a hot flash?"

"No, a flashback. You know, we've done this before."

"Done what?"

"Slept on the sand next to a river."

"Yeah, last night and the night before that," I replied.

"No, I'm talking about thirty-six years ago, on our first date. The sandbar party. Don't tell me you've forgotten our first date."

"That was forever ago."

"Remember how you told me that *all* of your fraternity brothers and their dates were going to sleep on the river once the party was over?" She giggled again. "And when the sun came up the next morning, we were the only ones on the sandbar. It was just you and me, sleeping on the sand next to the Kansas River."

"I've never forgotten that moment."

"Do you remember what woke us up?"

"Yeah, a guy was walking his German Shepard along the beach and it jumped on you and started licking your face. You thought it was a wolf."

By the light of the Milky Way I could see Karen smiling as she looked up at the sky. She asked, "You know what I remember most about that date?"

"Thinking you were being attacked by a wolf?"

"No. I remember when you called me and asked me to go to the bonfire party with you and you brought up the subject of spending the night on the beach. You were kind of nervously, sweetly awkward as you assured me that we would just be *sleeping* on the beach, nothing else."

"Once a gentleman, always a gentleman," I said.

"Yep. You know," she paused while reaching over and patting me until she found my hand, "Because of you, my life has been one big adventure. We've done things that I never would have done on my own. And yes, you've almost gotten me killed a few times, but I wouldn't have it any other way. It's been an incredible life with you."

"It's not over yet," I replied, squeezing her hand. "There are a few more imaginary pieces of paper in your imaginary bucket. We have a lot of adventures left, you and I."

"I'm glad about that," she said sleepily. There was nothing but the sound of the river for a few minutes, and then I heard a faint, "I love you."

"I love you too, Sweetie," I said, as I tucked her arm back into her sleeping bag and zipped it up tight.

The chair circle after dinner with the fire pit in the middle.

DAY FIVE

Day five on the river was a Tuesday, not that we knew it. By then we'd lost track of what day of the week it was. It was a beautiful morning, just like all of our mornings on the river. We'd been blessed with near-perfect weather the entire trip.

We had another leisurely morning before it was time to shove off. The crew was making breakfast while a couple of the women were doing yoga stretches by the river. Mark was circling us doing lunges with a resistance band. He was training for an Ironman. Karen and I were in the chair circle having coffee when I saw Lolly walking toward us. She was coming from the latrine area and had a bandana wrapped around her face. She looked like a bandit from an old Western movie. "Did you just rob the groover?" I asked. "Tell us the truth and we'll go easy on you."

"The groover stinks!" she complained. "Andrew! We need a new groover!"

Andrew took another sip of his coffee and said calmly, "I think the one we're using has another day or two left in it."

"Have you seen it? Have you smelled it? Please!" she pleaded.

"I'll check it out, but we have another twelve or thirteen days left on the river and only so much groover capacity. We need to make this one last as long as we can," he said.

Lolly shivered and looked our way, "Have you seen the groover?"

"It's not that bad," I said.

"It's horrible," she replied.

"Well, it is a little unpleasant, but only for sixty seconds a day. That's a small price to pay for being down here on this amazing trip," I said.

"We need a new groover," she said. "Maybe if I ask Eric…" she marched off with a sense of purpose.

It was our turn to ride with Rondo in his dory the *Shoshone*. Iain and Gill joined us. Rondo was in good physical condition, and I guessed he had many years left as a boatman, but he had made a few comments in the previous days suggesting that this might be his last trip as a professional dory boatman. Whenever someone would bring up the topic of his possible retirement, he would quickly change the subject. Maybe he was unsure about whether to hang up the oars after this trip or maybe he knew it was his last and didn't want to talk about it.

We began the day at mile 65 and had a calm morning on the river for the first eight miles. At mile 73 we ran through Unkar Rapid. Based on Rondo's reaction when we went through the rapid, I took it that Unkar was rougher than he had expected it to be. We made it through OK, but I was surprised at how energetically he was instructing us to bail as we navigated through the white water. It's possible he was testing us and getting us ready for the main event of the day, Hance Rapid, just past mile 77.

Hance would be the biggest rapid we would experience on the trip. It's rated a 7-8 on the 1 to 10 scale and drops thirty feet. As is often the case with many of the large rapids, Eric decided to beach our flotilla on the shallow beach at mile 77 so the boatmen could scout the rapid beforehand.

As soon as the crew securely tethered the boats to the shore, Eric led the boatmen along a trail through the bushes and over a jumble of boulders to a vantage point where they could see Hance Rapid downstream. The established trail was evidence that scouting Hance is a common practice amongst boatmen. Eric was a little surprised that all of the passengers followed. Our group had a lot of energy, like puppies wanting to play. Once the passengers realized that the trail only went to the scouting spot, several started scrambling up the side of a cliff. Eric hollered in our direction, "Hey, you guys need to be careful over there. Those rocks are loose. Make sure you don't start a rockslide." I think what he meant to say was, "You guys need to go back to the boats and try not to get killed while we figure this out."

Our boatmen had floated the Colorado countless times before, but they still approached each rapid with caution and respect. No matter how much experience they had with a particular rapid, the conditions are never the same. They spent a lot of time discussing their strategy. A couple of the male passengers, who had experience piloting drift boats, joined the discussion about how to run the rapid.

I was one of the passengers who had been messing around on the loose rocks. After scraping my legs a couple of times on sharp boulders, I made my way back to the group looking at the rapid. I said to John, "If it were up to me, I'd enter the rapid way on the left side of the river and hug the shoreline to avoid the rough water in the middle of the channel."

He replied, "That's exactly the opposite of what Eric suggested they do. He said the left side is no man's land. The boats would be caught in the eddies over there and might never come out."

"So, what does he suggest?"

"See the big hole just to the right of center?"

"The one that looks like it would swallow a boat twice the size of one of our dories?"

"Yes, that one. We're going to start by going into that hole."

"Did Eric say anything about taking a vote? I'm not sure it's a good idea to row our boat into that giant hole on purpose."

"They know what they're doing. They've run this rapid

before. So, we enter the hole, and if we don't get sucked to the bottom of the river, the plan is to then paddle hard to try to reach the duck pond."

"What's a duck pond?"

"It's that small area in the center of the rapid where the water is flat."

"I see it. It's about ten feet wide. The plan is to try to hit that spot?"

"Yes, and if they make it to that spot, they can pivot and push hard to the left so they can enter the tongue on the left side. If they do that, they'll be able to ride it to the end of the rapid."

"I don't see a tongue."

"It's that wave in the middle that looks like a tongue."

"Still don't see it."

"You will when we go through it."

We hiked back to where the dories were parked, climbed aboard and dug our helmets out of the hatches. I was no longer putting on my rain gear for the big rapids. Rain gear or not, I always got thoroughly soaked, and as soon as we made it through the rapid, the sun would warm me quickly.

For Hance, even the boatmen put on helmets. I don't recall whether they had worn helmets on previous rapids or not. By their demeanor, I could tell they were taking this run more seriously than the ones before.

I heard Karen in the back of the boat say, "I hope we don't flip. Please, God, don't let us flip."

I responded jokingly, "What are you worried about, it's a great day for a swim."

Karen and I bantered like that for a few more rounds, and then Rondo interrupted, "That's enough of that. Let's keep it positive. When we are on the river, we only talk positively." I respected his point; there was no reason to introduce a negative vibe.

When we pushed off from the shore and Rondo straightened the dory in the river channel, he explained the strategy for running the rapid. It was just as John had told me. "I need everyone to hold on tight when we go into the hole. When we come out of it and get to the flat spot, I need everyone to bail as fast as they can. I'll only have a few seconds to change directions, and I need the boat to be as light as possible." He said this in a tone that we understood wasn't merely a suggestion; it was a command from the captain. Message received.

As usual, Eric was piloting the lead dory, the *Marble Canyon*. We were second in line. Rondo held the *Shoshone* a hundred yards or so back from Eric to give him some space. This also allowed Rondo time to get a good view of Eric's run and to learn any last bits of information before we made our approach.

I was sitting in the front of our dory, so I could see Eric, standing in the center of his boat as it glided toward the rapid. He was getting one last look before going in. I remember thinking, as I watched Eric approach the rapid, that the water looked like it was flowing more steeply downhill than the rapids earlier in the trip. It was.

Eric sat down and made a few final steering paddles. Then his dory disappeared. From our angle it looked like the *Marble Canyon* was no longer on the river; it was just gone. "Oh shit!" I thought to myself. That's a bigger hole than it looked like from the shore. No wonder the boatmen had discussed strategy for so long. A couple of seconds later we saw the *Marble Canyon* shoot up as it hit the downstream side of the hole. I didn't see what happened next. I was looking at Iain with wide eyes. I said, "We're next buddy. Hold on!" We both grabbed the gunwales and squeezed tightly.

Rondo guided the dory to the exact spot where he wanted to enter the rapid. When we reached a point about fifty feet from the top of the hole, the river took control. It was the point of no return, and all of us, Rondo included, were just holding on for dear life. The power of the river's current was impressive. Our speed accelerated gradually at first, and then picked up quickly until it felt like we went into a free fall. The fall ended with a bang at the bottom of the hole. The river tossed the dory in all directions. Rondo paddled furiously, and within seconds we were on the duck pond. "Bail!" he yelled.

I reached for my bailing jug and smacked heads with Iain. He was bailing like a mad man. His scoops were so fast I couldn't time mine to keep from banging into him. I lifted my legs and put them on the deck in front of us to stay out of his way. He had the footwell cleared in no time. "Good job!" yelled Rondo, "It's not over yet, hold on!"

The water rodeo resumed. I still couldn't tell where the tongue was, but Rondo seemed to have the boat right where he wanted it. He was making big, lunging paddles between waves. He hollered in our direction, "I need you to lean into that last big wave. I'll tell you when."

By then, Iain and I had gotten the hang of high siding; we were ready. Our dory passed through a couple of large waves head on. The third wave was the biggest. Rondo shouted, "This is it!" That's all he needed to say. Iain and I stood up and pushed all of our weight onto the front deck of the boat as it hit the wave and went vertical. Water came over the bow and drenched us, but the mass of our bodies was enough to keep the dory from flipping backward. Once we reached the back side of the wave, I heard shrieks and peals of laughter from Karen and Gill as the stern lifted high out of the water. What a thrill! We made it through Hance Rapid right side up.

It was over as fast as it had started. We were back on flat water peacefully floating downstream. Rondo turned the *Shoshone* 90 degrees so we had a good view of the boats behind us navigating the rapid we'd just come through. As I watched, I could see all of the passengers laughing uncontrollably as the river tossed them about. It *was* turning into the best trip of all time.

All the boats in our group made it through Hance without incident. There were a couple of small rapids just past Hance that we ran with relative ease. The boats closed ranks as we were getting ready to pull over and set up for lunch. Eric yelled back in our direction, "Rondo! Paddle!" He was pointing to the left bank of the river. "Uh-oh," Rondo said. He turned the dory around and for a brief stretch paddled upstream. In the water was a blue paddle with a yellow fin. It looked like it belonged to a raft group. Rondo pulled close, and I snagged the paddle out of the water. "Does this go into your collection of paddles?" I asked.

"No, we'll probably see those folks later this afternoon. I'm surprised there's nothing else of theirs in the water."

His instincts were correct. A few minutes later we landed the dories on a small beach that had a backdrop of large boulders behind it. Four rafts were already tied up on the shore when we arrived. The rocks were covered with clothes drying in the sun. It looked like a garage sale. Apparently, the rafters had flipped somewhere upstream. Rondo found the group's leader at the end of the beach, returned the paddle, and then he stayed and talked with him for another fifteen minutes or so. From where we stood it didn't look like a back-slapping, cheery "can you believe what just happened to us" discussion; it was more solemn. We never learned what happened to the group. All Rondo said when he came back was, "They're fine." We could tell from the demeanor of the rafters that something had gone wrong, something more than just a raft flipping, and they were pissed. They were also in no mood to visit. They took off before our crew set up the lunch tables and hand washing station.

We felt a sense of relief after making it through Hance Rapid without any difficulties: none of the boats had flipped or hit a rock, and no one fell out. While we were eating lunch, one of the passengers said, "We can celebrate now. We've made it through the hardest rapids of the trip." Our premature merriment didn't sit well with one of the boatmen, "We still have Sockdolager this afternoon and Grapevine tomorrow. We need to stay focused. Let's finish strong and celebrate when we get to Phantom Ranch." Having observed the crew for four days, I had picked up on a subtle characteristic of theirs: they were superstitious.

About a mile downstream from where we ate lunch was

Sockdolager Rapid. It was rougher than I thought it would be, but our luck held and the boatmen's skill got us through without incident.

Phill bow-riding the *Shoshone* with Rondo at the oars. He got the nickname "touchdown Rogerson" on the trip. I'm not sure who that is in the back in full rain gear.

GRAPEVINE CAMP

There was plenty of daylight left when we stopped just shy of mile 82 for the night. Grapevine was the name of our campsite, which sat between Cottonwood Creek to the east and Grapevine Creek to the west. The site was a large, flat, sandy area that looked like the National Park Service put it there on purpose. A massive granite cliff with a slight overhang protected the site on the south side giving it a cozy feel. It was a treat for us to be able to spend the night there because the National Park Service only allows tours doing passenger exchanges to camp at sites within the ten-mile stretch just before Phantom Ranch.

Many river guides don't like passenger exchanges. With five days under their belts, everyone is settled into a routine. By then they've learned their passengers' fitness levels and interests so they can plan the day's activities accordingly. And the passengers have acclimated to the customs of river life. Just when everyone has forgotten what his or her old life was like and reaches that, "I could live like this forever" feeling, it's time to plunge back into civilization. It would have been nice to have at least another day or two before the trip was over, but the guide companies don't get to decide where the passenger exchange takes place. Phantom Ranch is the only feasible spot on the river.

It's not ideal for the new passengers either. One of our guides said to us, "So, there's a whole new group that spends the night on the South Rim. Then, they have to get up before sunrise and hike ten miles down to Phantom Ranch so we can shove off in time to make our campsite for the night. Some of them have never done a physical activity that strenuous before, so the hike wipes them out by the time they make it to the dories. They sit in the sand and eat a sandwich while we give them a quick safety briefing and as soon as we get on the river we have to run one of the most difficult rapids of the trip. By the first night, the new group is shell-shocked."

The storms that brought rain and flooding before our trip had stayed away since we launched at Lees Ferry. I could tell by the shape of the clouds that rain might be back soon. Once the boats were unloaded, Karen and I chose a patch of sand that would be our home for the evening. We were hoping to sleep under the stars for one more night. It was tempting to take our chances and leave our tent unassembled, but I put it up to be on the safe side. There are few things worse than trying to put up a tent in the midst of a downpour in the middle of the night while all of your stuff is getting soaked. That's not a relationship building activity Karen and I need to experience.

The main reason for getting to our site so early in the afternoon was to hike above the Grapevine campsite. The boatmen were eagerly looking forward to this hike, even more so than the other hikes we'd done that week.

On those earlier hikes, I noticed the boatmen wearing sandals rather than tennis shoes or hiking boots. When I pointed this out on the second day of the trip, one of them replied, "Well, there is a saying that a passenger came up with years ago. It goes something like, 'If the boatmen are barefoot, you should wear sandals. If the boatmen are wearing sandals, you should wear hiking boots. If the boatmen are wearing hiking boots, you shouldn't go.' " For the Grapevine hike the boatmen strapped on their hiking boots.

I asked one of the boatmen, "No sandals today?"

"No sandals. This hike is a little more difficult than the others."

Only a handful of passengers and crew stayed in camp while we hiked. Karen stayed behind, saying she was conserving her energy for the hike out of the canyon. As Eric led the way, I was curious as to why he was walking toward our tent. I'd checked out the terrain behind our sleeping area; it was a dead end. There was nothing back there except a rock-strewn ravine that was nearly vertical. That's where Eric was heading.

"It's not a trail," Eric said. "It's a route."

I didn't understand what that meant. I guess it was an inside joke amongst the boatmen because several times during our outing one would say, "It's not a trail." And another boatman would reply "It's a route." I don't know the difference between a trail and a route, but I can tell you the path—let's call it a path—was treacherous.

Karen and I have hiked difficult trails before. This was the most difficult I'd ever done, not only because of the physical effort required, but also because the footing was loose and the path steep. I'm surprised no one accidentally kicked a boulder down on the hiker below them or started a rockslide.

Despite the sketchy conditions, we all made it to the top of the ravine without anyone getting hurt. I don't know the exact elevation gain of our hike through the ravine, but it felt like about a 500-foot gain. When we got to the top, the terrain leveled, and we continued hiking another quarter of a mile to an overlook.

From the vista we could see the Tonto Trail, which, if you could find a way to get to it, would lead you to trails that go all the way to the South Rim. We could also look west along the Colorado River and see glimpses of Grapevine Rapid that we would run the next day.

Being up there gave us a sense of what it would have been like if we were on the Powell Expedition and had been sent on a reconnaissance mission to find a route out of the canyon. A person could get disoriented quickly in the mess of side canyons, ravines, and plateaus. It was a jumble up there, but also beautiful.

We poked around up top for a while looking over the sides of drop-offs and taking panoramic photos. When we started back down toward camp we found that going down was more treacherous than coming up. There were a couple of times I came to dead ends and had to climb back up the hill to re-find the path. It was curious how easy it was to lose the trail even though there were twenty people in front of me to follow. I was relieved to get back to the flat sand of the campsite, but also glad I'd done the hike.

Karen was sitting in the chair circle with JB, Aya, and Debi when we got back. JB was regaling them with 'back in the day' stories. We could sense the end of the trip nearing, and our night at Grapevine would be our last chance to draw out the river tales from our seasoned crew. JB was an exceptional source of information about the formative days of dory expeditions through the Grand Canyon.

When I got to the chair circle, I caught the end of one of JB's stories about his early days on the river. I heard him say, "After we got my broken dory to shore and Martin looked at the damage, he said to me, 'Well, JB, these boats have been banged up like this before, just never all at once.' We laughed about that for the next forty years."

Eric retrieved a copy of the *boatman's quarterly review* from the hatch of his dory and brought it to the chair circle. The issue featured Martin Litton with a photo of him on the cover. It looked as if it had been taken when he was in his 70s or 80s. You could see the decades Litton spent in the canyon on his weathered face. His white hair and beard were striking. Eric stood up and said, "Hey, everyone. Do you mind if I read some of this article out loud to the group? It's about the life of Martin Litton, and it's really important to know about everything he did to preserve this wonderful place for all of us."

No one objected, and Eric read for a good twenty minutes or so. A couple of times he stopped to make sure that he wasn't boring the group, and to ask permission to keep going. We all appreciated Eric's reading and encouraged him to continue. At one point he read a quote of Litton's from the article, "The best way for people to understand how important it is to have the bottom of the Grand Canyon preserved, and have its aquatic life saved, and its riparian zone with the beauty that's there, kept, is perhaps to have them on that river and let them feel the way it stirs and rumbles and moves you along at its own pace, and to sense the kind of 'life' the river has. It has a tremendous force and appeal that I can't describe."

You could see in his face how much Eric revered Litton. And even though Eric wasn't near the age Litton was when the cover photo had been taken, he was even beginning to look like the elder Litton.

When he was done reading the article to us, Eric said, "You guys might want to sign up for this journal. You don't have to be a boatman to subscribe, and the money goes to a good cause. A group called the Grand Canyon River Guides puts it out. Their purpose is to, well, it says right here, I'll read it to you, 'Protecting (the) Grand Canyon, setting the highest standards for the river profession, celebrating the unique spirit of the river community, (and) providing the best possible river experience.' Now that's something worthwhile to support, don't you think?"

One impression I took away from our Grand Canyon river trip experience was that the people who put on these trips take their role as stewards of the canyon seriously. Sure, providing float trips is a moneymaker for the concessionaires, but I felt they were sincere in their desire to keep the canyon as pristine as possible and to educate us on the value of preserving and protecting it for future visitors. It was inspiring to see how much the crew respected the river and the people who came before them who had protected it. We were fortunate to get this crew. They made us feel as if we

Matt and Karen Smith

had a connection—albeit a degree or two removed—to those early days of the river's exploration.

Eric finished reading, and we were milling around the kitchen area as the crew prepared dinner when I saw Craig with another issue of the *boatman's quarterly review* in his hand. A group of passengers gathered around Craig as he thumbed through the pages. On the cover was a photo of a handsome young man with a dark, full beard. He was wearing a leather safari hat and mirrored sunglasses. "Who's that?" I asked. Craig gave me a sideways look and then held the cover out so I could see it clearly. That's when I noticed the big "Q" on the cover. Craig was holding the cover of the magazine next to Q's face, who was standing two feet from us. "Oh, I see. Q, you were a sharp looking guy back then. I mean, you *are* a sharp looking guy. I mean—never mind—anyone need a beer?"

When we'd all finished dinner, the crew placed the firebox from the grill in the center of the chair circle so we could have a campfire for our last night. It was routine for Eric to ask one of the crew to talk after dinner: one night Q gave us a history lesson about the Colorado River, and another night JB told us about his years of experience as a boatman. I didn't know what the evening talk would be about that night, but I wanted to make sure the passengers had an opportunity to speak. I said to Eric during dinner, "If it's alright with you, the passengers and I would like some time after dinner to talk to the group while everyone, especially the crew, is still around the circle."

Craig and I waited until everyone was finished with dessert and had a comfortable spot to sit around the fire. We brought one of the blue tarps, placed it inside the chair circle and brushed the sand off of it. On top of the tarp, we put the gifts that each of the couples had brought as a thank you for the crew. There were ten gifts, one for each crewmember.

The gifts were simple gestures of our thanks to the crew. On the tarp were a couple of t-shirts, a Seattle Seahawks beanie, a multi-purpose camping tool, a belt buckle from

206

Stockman's bar (my gift)—they were small items, but fun. I made sure Eric knew before we started that these gifts were not our sole gratuity for the crew. Our research before we left home suggested that each person tip the crew between 5% and 10% of the cost of the trip. That amount, of course, depends on the level of service you feel the crew provided. One-by-one we each discretely gave Eric our gratuity. Another job of the leader is to collect the tip money and divvy it up amongst the crew.

I joined Craig in the center of the chair circle, and we each said a few words of thanks to the crew on behalf of the passengers. And then it was time to hand out the gifts. Rather than trying to decide which crewmember would receive which gift, we made it a white elephant: one person selects a gift and then it's the next person's turn. The second person can steal the first person's gift or choose a new gift, and so on.

We came up with a pecking order as to when each crewmember got to choose a gift that favored seniority. In a game like this, it's better to be one of the last to select a gift. The white elephant took much longer than we'd planned, but it was a lot of fun. White elephants can get nasty; B had the gift she chose stolen five different times, but in the end, she left with the Seahawks beanie, the gift she'd wanted the most in the first place. Andrew was stuck with a t-shirt that didn't fit. The next morning though, John gave Andrew an extra Stockman's Bar t-shirt that he had brought that was just Andrew's size.

The convivial mood must have inspired Andy. He got his guitar and banjo out of his dory, pulled his folding chair close to the fire and began playing. It was a perfect night. At that moment, every one of us would have agreed to continue the trip for the next ten days if that were an option.

It was getting late, at least according to river time, but Andy showed no signs of slowing. I think he would have played all night had the rain not started. At first, it was a sprinkle. We looked at each other as if to ask, "Is this going to turn into something more, or just blow over?" Andy never hesitated and kept playing. Slowly the rain got heavier, and then the wind picked up. All at once everyone made a mad dash for cover. Andy looked up, shrugged his shoulders, and slowly packed up his instruments and stowed them.

All of the passengers had set up tents earlier in the day, having heard there was a slight chance of rain. But most of the crew had still planned on sleeping on the decks of their boats. It was too dark and windy to try to set up a tent, so everyone without shelter pulled his or her sleeping gear up against the cliff at the back of the campsite. Fortunately, the granite wall had a slight overhang that kept them dry.

We all scurried to get into our tents. Even though Karen and I had put up our tent earlier, most of our stuff was still scattered across our tarps. We did our best to find our clothes and put them under the rain fly of our tent before they got soaked.

At the precise moment when everyone had completed their frantic gathering of stuff and dove into their tents bringing with them a couple of shoes full of sand, the rain ended. It didn't rain a drop the rest of the night. Karen and I laid in our tent wide-awake, slightly damp with our hearts racing, wondering if we should move outside the tent to sleep. No one knew if the rain would come back, and moving our pads and sleeping bags out of the tent would be a hassle, so we stayed inside our muggy tent.

A few feet away we could hear John and Lolly trying to get comfortable in their tent. Apparently, in their hurry to get out of the rain, they hadn't oriented their tent or sleeping bags the way Lolly wanted. "John, move over!" we heard.

"Where do you want me to go? I'm up against the side of the tent."

"Well, I'm rolling toward the middle. I can't sleep like this."

"Lolly! You're on my arm."

"We need to move the tent."

"We're not moving the tent."

Their back-and-forth didn't sound like it was going to end any time soon, so Karen waited about five minutes, and then yelled, "Andersons! We can hear every word you're saying."

We heard giggling for a minute, and then it started again.

"John!"

"Lolly!"

"John!"

"Lolly! You can sleep outside if you don't like it."

For the sake of full disclosure, we heard a lot of laughing between their grumbles.

I said in a loud voice, "Karen, next time, we should wait until John and Lolly claim their sleeping area before we decide where to sleep for the night."

We heard John say, "You guys can move. There's plenty of open area by the groover."

Fortunately, sort of, the next sound I heard from their tent was the two of them snoring. "How can they do that?" I asked Karen. "Keep us up with their bickering and then fall asleep that fast." Karen's response was a snore. The latrine area sounded good right about then.

Q

Grapevine Camp

Eric reading about the life of Martin Litton from the
boatmen's quarterly review.

DAY SIX

The next morning was sunny, and the skies were clear. It was as if the rain from the night before was a figment of our imagination. The crew moved at a relaxed pace; Phantom Ranch was a mere six miles downstream, so our time on the river would be relatively short. Everyone took his or her time getting ready.

Once the passengers had packed their sleep kits and brought them to the cargo boats, Eric and a couple of other crewmembers began the thankless job of opening each kit, changing the pillow cases and sleeping bag liners, shaking all of the sand out and neatly re-packing everything back into the blue dry bags. That night, the new passengers who rented sleep kits would be using the kits we'd used that week. Eric was responsible for making sure they each got a fresh kit.

While Eric was taking care of his business, Andy and Betsy put the rest of us to work. Before the mess area was broken down and packed onto the rafts, they set up a sandwich making assembly line. I missed the first part of their instructions. All I heard was Andy say, "Everyone needs to make two sandwiches, one for you and one for a friend." I thought that was odd, "Why are we making sandwiches for a friend? I don't have a friend," I thought to myself.

By the time I got to the table, the sandwich fixins were

slim. I made my two each with only one thin slice of salami and a dash of mustard. I followed everyone else's lead and put each sandwich in a paper bag along with a granola bar and a couple of cookies. Everyone was handing one of their bags to Andy and packing the other in their small dry bag. "Why is Andy collecting half of the sandwiches?" I asked Karen.

"Those are for the new passengers. When they get to the river after hiking down the canyon this morning, it'll be time for lunch. We were making their sack lunches," she replied.

"Uh-oh, I hope my 'friend' isn't very hungry. I went a little lean on the salami."

"I wouldn't worry about it," Karen said. "When we meet the new passengers we'll tell them that John made all of the sandwiches."

With the lunches made and the sleep kits refreshed, we were ready to pack up and bug out. Andrew was standing by the hand wash station when he hollered, "Last call for the groover!" He'd done that every morning on the river, and every morning a couple of people came running toward the latrine. Once everyone had finished his or her groover business, Andrew did his daily duty of hauling the groover onto his raft. Before he put it into the hold, he paused and yelled to the group standing on the beach, "I just want you to know that this is the last time I'm taking any of your shit!" We all laughed.

It was a little sad to shout our final Dories, Ho! when we pushed off the shore of Grapevine camp. John and Lolly partnered with us in Andre's dory for the home stretch. For the first time all week, Karen and I sat next to each other in the front of the boat. The other times, the men sat in the front, and the women sat in the back. The gals had insisted; they thought they wouldn't get as wet back there. But over the course of the week, the passengers sitting in the back of the dories took as many waves as those sitting up front.

Grapevine Rapid was a hoot: big waves, a high side or two, lots of bailing, and uncontrollable laughter. All the boats made it through without incident, same for Zoroaster Rapid a couple of miles downstream. In fact, none of the boats experienced any accidents or flips during the entire trip.

In early summer of the following year, Karen, Lolly, John and I traveled to New Mexico to visit several national parks. While we were in Sante Fe, we had dinner with Betsy. It was fun to catch up with her and reminisce about our trip. We asked her how the second half had gone and she told us that they had made it through the rest of the trip without any boating accidents. Eric's first time piloting the *Marble Canyon* was a golden run.

"But there was a scary incident. We experienced a rockfall in camp toward the end of the trip."

"What happened?" Karen asked. We weren't aware of the gravity of what Betsy had just told us until she explained further.

"A bunch of rocks fell around our campsite early one morning as we were just waking up."

"Were they big rocks?" we asked.

"Big enough. Some of them had to weigh at least a couple hundred pounds."

"Did anyone get hurt?"

"Just me. I was the only one who got hit."

"That's terrible," Karen said. "Are you OK?"

"Yeah, I still have a mark on my leg where the rock hit me. It'll never go away."

"So, where were you when this happened?"

"We'd camped at Fern Glen, about eleven miles upriver from Lava Falls. In fact, that was the day we would go through Lava Falls. It was early in the morning, but most everyone was up and around. I was still in my sleeping bag when it happened. I didn't sleep well the night before because my feet were a little bit higher than my head. I kept thinking all night I should flip around and sleep the other way, but I never did. It was a good thing I didn't. The rock landed on my lower leg. It was about the size of a pumpkin. If it had hit me in the head, I would have been a goner."

"Wow. You're lucky to be here, Betsy," Lolly said.

"I know, very lucky. It was written about in the latest *boatman's quarterly review*, the spring 2017 edition. I brought my copy to give you guys. Q wrote a couple of pages describing what happened and Andre took some pictures. One of the rocks hit a chair in the chair circle. If someone had been sitting in that chair, they would have been hurt badly. It really freaked us out."

"What did you do once the rock hit you?"

"I started crawling as fast as I could toward the cliff. I was still in my sleeping bag. Most people would think to move away from the cliff, but in a rockfall, you want to move closer to it. As the rocks fall, they're bouncing off the cliff and other rocks. They're more likely to land away from the base of the cliff, which is what happened. Rondo was in the kitchen area taking cover under a table and yelled for everyone to get to the cliff."

"Do you know how it started?"

"We don't know for sure. Our camp was under a cliff, so the rocks were falling a long way before they reached us. One of the guys thought that maybe a bighorn sheep had started a slide way above us. You know, if they kick one rock downhill and it hits another, that's enough to start a slide. It was really scary for a few moments."

"Wow, you're lucky no one else got hurt."

"Oh, I know. Andy, B, and Maia were on their boats at the time, and rocks landed close enough that the water from the impacts splashed them. One big rock landed right between two of the dories. Someone could have been hurt seriously. And if one of the dories had gotten hit by a big rock, I don't know what we would have done."

Betsy gave me her copy of the *boatman's quarterly review*, so we could read about it and circulate the magazine amongst the other couples. Of all of the things we'd worried might happen to us on the trip, a rockfall wasn't one of them.

By mile 86, the river was dead calm. We were in the basement of the canyon. Shiny black boulders lined the shore. There were streaks of red and pink in the rocks. The mostly-black rock was Vishnu Schist, and the pink streaked rock was Zoroaster Granite. They're called "basement rocks" because they're the oldest and hardest rocks the Colorado River carved through. They are the bedrock of much of North America, and the bottom of the Grand Canyon is one of, if not *the*, best place to see them.

A couple of billion years ago the material from which these rocks were made accumulated and became rock. Over time, heat and pressure caused it to change and harden further. Now, exposed by the river, they're beautiful. They can also be dangerously sharp if you try to pound a tent stake into the ground with one.

"Vishnu Schist," I said to Karen.

"What's Vishnu Schist?"

"Those black, shiny rocks over there."

"How do you know?"

"I remember it from the Trail of Time walk on the South Rim. Andre, is that Vishnu Schist?" I asked pointing to an enormous, jagged boulder sitting half in the river, half on the shore.

"Yep, sure is."

Andre, being a geologist, was in his happy place floating through this open-air time capsule of rock history. I have to admit, I'm not much interested in the geology of the Grand Canyon. That seems sacrilegious to say, but I can't help it. Don't get me wrong. The canyon is one of the most beautiful and peaceful places on earth. The landscape and rock formations are stunning, the colors sublime. I just can't make myself care about whether a certain layer of rock is 250 million years old or a billion.

But I love Vishnu Schist. I'd like to have a few big boulders of it in our backyard around our patio. When guests come over, I would tell them how it formed deep in the earth. "It's metamorphic you see. It metamorphosized." That's what I would say, and they would be impressed. Karen thinks I just like saying the name.

"Vishnu Schist. It sounds like I'm swearing in another language doesn't it?" I said to Karen.

"Are you expecting an answer, or just bored and saying whatever comes into your head?"

"I'm trying to show some interest in the geology of the canyon, so Andre doesn't think we're idiots."

"He's been traveling with us for a week, he already knows."

The thing that makes it hard for me to care more about the geology is that I can't tell one rock layer from the next, except for the Vishnu Schist. All week, the boatmen would announce each new rock formation as we would pass it along the river. On our first day, Andy said to us, "Here's where the Hermit Shale makes its first appearance. Do you see? Right below that band of Coconino Sandstone?" He said this while motioning with his head toward a 500-foot cliff of rock that all looked the same.

"Where was that, Andy?" I asked.

"Right there, see? There's a band of limestone. Just below that is the Coconino Sandstone. And right below that is the shale."

"Oh, the Coconino Limestone. I see it now."

"Coconino Sandstone," he said patiently.

"Sandstone, that's what I meant. Definitely sandstone."

I tried to act as if I cared, but I'm sure it was obvious I wasn't following along. Most of the time I thought they were playing a joke on us. Later in the week, one of the boatmen said, "The Redwall Limestone isn't truly red. The red comes from the rock that sits above it. The red bleeds down and stains the rocks below." I'll take their word for it.

The names of the rocks are fun though. They sound exotic, like the names of movie stars. As we floated through the peaceful last mile of the trip, I said to Karen, "I could imagine a blockbuster film starring Hermit Shale and Vishnu Schist, couldn't you?"

"That would be a good name for a dog, Hermit Shale. A small geeky dog with glasses," she said.

"You just described Mr. Peabody."

"Yes! Make that Hermit Peabody Shale."

"You know what worries me?" I said. "If something happened to me, I think you might just rescue a dog so that you could name him Hermit P. Shale."

"You're probably right."

"Let's agree we're not getting a dog, but if we ever have a fourth child, we'll name him Coconino, or Coconina if it's a girl. She'll be a movie star."

"I think that ship has sailed, Sweetie," Karen said.

This is where my mind goes when the subject of geology comes up.

If Andre was able to hear our conversation, he didn't give any indication. He was probably thinking to himself, "Let's move it along, Eric. I need to get these morons off my dory."

Andrew on his raft.

The *Black Canyon* with Andre at the oars.

PHANTOM RANCH

At mile 88, we saw our first meaningful sign of civilization in five days: the Kaibab Suspension Bridge. It was a shock to see a bridge across the river. My first thought was, "What is that doing down here at the bottom of the canyon?" I had become accustomed to the pristine backcountry. The bridge marked the beginning of our return to our previous life.

Also known as the Black Bridge (because it's black), it was built in 1928. The completion of the bridge eased travel across the river at Bright Angel Creek. Before it was built, people and livestock had to ride in open-air metal cages suspended from cables above the river to get from one side to the other. Once in a cage, the operator would pull it across the river. I read a story about Teddy Roosevelt insisting that he pull himself across the river in one of those metal cages when he visited the area. The new bridge changed the river crossing experience from a harrowing experience to a safe and convenient stroll.

My favorite detail about the building of the Kaibab Suspension Bridge is how the National Park Service got the 550-foot support cables from the rim of the canyon to the river. Each cable weighed about a ton. They recruited Havasupai men to carry the cables down the trail. Forty-two men, in unison, would pick up one of the cables and walk it down to the river. There are photos of them doing this; the cable snaked and bent as they wound their way to the bottom.

Another third of a mile downstream is the Bright Angel Suspension Bridge, also known as the Silver Bridge (because it's silver). The downriver bridge is the newer of the two; it was built in 1970 to support the water pipeline that runs from Roaring Springs, north of the river, to the South Rim. Now, both bridges provide enough passage for the large volume of hikers to cross easily while also allowing plenty of room for mule traffic. Generally, mules use the Kaibab Suspension Bridge, and hikers are free to use either.

The mouth of Bright Angel Creek sits between the two suspension bridges. Where the creek meets the Colorado River, there is a broad delta that's mostly covered with scrubby vegetation. On the east side of the delta, there's a narrow boat beach where, at a little past 11:00 am, we landed for the last time.

As we got close to the shore, we could see some of the new passengers waiting at the beach. "Fresh meat," Karen said.

"I bet they smell like soap," I replied.

"Yeah, they look pretty clean." Karen paused for a moment and then said to me, "I think we should tell Eric to give the new group a quick look over and if he spots any duds, like whiners or complainers, he should kick them out, and we'll take their spot on the second half of the trip."

"He would just tell them, 'Sorry, you're out, there's been a change of plans, call the office, and they'll issue you a refund.' Is that what you're imagining?"

"No, he wouldn't just say 'you're out.' He could gather them around and tell them they have to clean out the groovers before they can shove off. Anyone who refuses wouldn't be allowed to go. He could say, 'It's in the fine print of the contract you signed, nothing I do about it.' "

"I think that's a really good idea. When we get off the boat, you should definitely suggest that to Eric. Just don't do it while I'm around," I said.

The new passengers had started their hike down at sunrise with just their daypacks. They only had to carry what they needed on the hike; mules brought down their heavier duffels, which held their clothes and other personal gear. We spoke with two young guys who looked to be in good physical condition. They said they were able to get down the trail in just a few hours, but others in their group weren't moving as quickly. We learned later that it took some of them seven hours to complete the hike to the river.

There wasn't a big "goodbye" scene when we got off the dories. There was a lot to do in a short amount of time. The crew had to offload all of our dry bags and make sure we took all of our stuff with us that we'd stowed in the dory hatches. Then, we had to take all of our gear out of the dry bags and fit it into the duffels we'd brought with us. With sixteen of us bumping into each other on that narrow beach, it turned into a comical fire drill:

"I can't find my dry bag, never mind, here it is."

"No, that one's mine."

"Then where's mine? Andrew! Andrew!"

"They're all on the beach somewhere, guys."

"OK. I have it now, thank you."

I tried to find my duffel that was inside my dry bag, but I was having a hard time. Since I hadn't needed it all week, it had worked its way to the bottom. I dumped everything out onto the sand. "Duffel bag. Duffel bag. Where is my duffel bag? Oh no, I think I forgot to pack my duffel bag."

"It's right here," Karen said, as she grabbed it off the top of my pile. She had a look of concern on her face like she was worried I was losing my mind.

I packed my duffel as full as I could and still had quite a bit of clothing left. The rest barely fit into my daypack. Phill stood over me and said, "Wow, that's a lot of stuff, Matt. Did you really think you'd need all of that on the river?" His duffel was hanging across his chest. I could see by the slack in the fabric that it was about half full.

"Don't worry about my stuff, Phill. Go bother someone else," I replied.

Once we had all of our gear ready to go, we said our rushed and awkward goodbyes to the crew. They were already busy preparing for the next group, but stopped long enough to exchange hugs. We all promised to stay in touch. Andy said, "We'll see you soon." Everyone says they'll "see you soon" when they say goodbye.

Karen replied, "Yes. We'll see you again, not sure when, but we promise. As a matter of fact, we want to do this trip again, but next time we're doing the entire length of the river. Maybe you could be one of the boatmen on our next trip. That way, we'd see you again in a couple of years."

Andy gave Karen a quizzical look, "A couple of years? We'll get together before then." I thought that was a nice thing for him to say. I hope we see all of them again someday. They're family now.

It was time to go. I strapped on my daypack and slung the duffel over my shoulder. It was a heavy load. Karen was standing next to me ready for the mile hike to Phantom Ranch. She was carrying her duffel across her front, messenger bag style just like Phill. "Are you sure you have everything?" she asked with a tone that someone would use when talking to a small child.

"I'm sure, but I do have one question for you, Sweetie. Why are you still wearing your life jacket? Do you like it so much you thought you'd take it with you? Maybe it's a new fashion trend you're trying to start. You might want to ask Eric though if it's OK that you take it. One of the new passengers might need it."

"Oh, crap. I didn't even know I was wearing it. How embarrassing."

"It's called Karma," I thought to myself.

A path led away from the beach toward Phantom Ranch. Along the path, a short distance from the beach, sat several wheelbarrows for passengers to use to haul their duffel bags. All but one of them had flat tires. We loaded the lone working wheelbarrow with our gear, but when we tried to push it along the trail it was more work than it was worth. The deep ruts on the trail made it nearly impossible. As it turned out, carrying all of our stuff to Phantom Ranch wasn't very difficult.

Phantom Ranch sits on fourteen acres about a half of a mile north of the Colorado River along Bright Angel Creek. In 1903, a man named David Rust set up a tourist tent camp in the area catering to adventure seekers and prospectors. After Teddy Roosevelt traveled to the spot in 1913, they named it Roosevelt Camp to honor his visit. In the early 1920s, the National Park Service granted the Fred Harvey Company concession rights to the camp. Soon after, Fred Harvey hired Mary Colter to design buildings for the site.

Colter designed the guest cabins to blend into the natural surroundings. Stones used to build them came from the creek nearby. Although nearly 100 years old, the buildings at Phantom Ranch look very similar to the way they looked when they were originally built. The timelessness of her designs is a testament to her skill as an architect.

The name Phantom Ranch was Colter's idea. She came up with it while she was working on the plans, drawing inspiration from nearby Phantom Creek. When Fred Harvey told her that the new cabins would be called Roosevelt Chalets, she protested. She threatened to withhold her designs and quit the project if they didn't accept her suggestion to name the newly renovated area Phantom Ranch. Apparently, she got her way.

Mary Colter was one of the few prominent female architects of the early 20th-century. In addition to creating the structures at Phantom Ranch, she designed several other buildings in Grand Canyon National Park including Hopi House, Bright Angel Lodge, Desert View Watchtower and Hermits Rest.

It would be hard for any visitor to Phantom Ranch today to imagine that there once was a swimming pool there. But it's true; in 1935, the Civilian Conservation Corps built a pool at Phantom Ranch. Many photos from the 1950s and 1960s show visitors relaxing around the pool area. It was a favorite activity for a couple of decades, but eventually became too much of a maintenance burden and was closed. Legend has it that unwanted furniture and debris were used to fill in the depression. I've read that you can still see where the pool once was between cabins number five and six by looking for the weedy depression in the landscape.

Phantom Ranch is the only place to stay overnight at the bottom of the canyon, other than campgrounds. The ranch has small cabins that accommodate two to four people and larger, group cabins that accommodate as many as ten. There are also beds available in dormitories: one male-only dorm and one female-only dorm, each with ten beds. The cabins have toilets and a sink with running water, but no showers. A separate building nearby houses the men's and women's showers. The dorms have their own showers.

About a quarter of a mile south of Phantom Ranch is Bright Angel Campground. The thirty-site campground is adjacent to the creek. Camping at the bottom of the canyon is a less expensive alternative than renting a cabin, or a backup if the cabins are all taken. However, during most times of the year, it's difficult to get either a cabin reservation or a camping permit due to the demand.

Eric and Andre walked with us to Phantom Ranch. Eric had to check in with the O.A.R.S. office by phone and try to get an update on when the rest of the new passengers might arrive at the river. I think Andre just wanted to get lemonade at the canteen.

The canteen is where meals are served; it also doubles as the reception desk for guests. When we arrived, our cabin, which was right next to the canteen, was available for us to move into. It was a group cabin that sleeps ten, so five couples shared that cabin and the other six in our group had beds in the dorms. We don't know how O.A.R.S. had decided who would sleep in the cabin and who would sleep in the dorms. Those who drew the dorm spots were disappointed to be separated from the group, but the next day we learned that everyone who slept in the dorms enjoyed their stay. Lolly said, "I think I liked the dorm better than I would have the cabin. There were no snoring men!"

We all stowed our gear in our respective sleeping areas and then grabbed clean clothes. It turned into a race for who could get to the showers first. I don't remember a shower ever feeling as good as the one I took that afternoon. The water was warm; it was clean; no one was watching me and making fun, it was heavenly. I got dressed and went back to the cabin smelling like soap.

Once we were all clean, we looked at each other as if to say, "Now what do we do for the next six hours?" Many of us decided to explore the area. Our original plan was to hike up the North Kaibab Trail to a slot canyon. We'd heard it was a fantastic hike, but the weather was threatening. The sky had turned cloudy, and it looked like it might rain. The storms from a week ago were returning. "We're not hiking in a slot canyon if there's any chance of rain," Karen said.

"I agree. It's not worth the risk," I replied.

Instead, everyone did their own thing, but stayed away from the canyons north of the ranch. Several couples went for hikes; Karen and I headed toward the Bright Angel Suspension Bridge. It was nice to not carry anything but water. We ate our thin salami sandwiches as we walked. The overcast sky kept the temperature down, which was a bonus. Every so often a gust of wind would sweep across the trail making me wonder if rain was coming soon.

We hiked across one of the suspension bridges and back on the other. The wind was getting stronger and the clouds darker. There was no doubt now, a storm was on its way, and it would be a gully washer. Karen and I started walking toward the cabin as the wind howled. The closer we got, the quicker we walked. For the last 100 feet, we ran through a downpour. Thunder and lightning rolled through the ranch as we sat safely in our cabin. "I feel so bad for the new passengers. They just got on the dories for their first time, and now they're out there on the river in this terrible storm," Karen said.

"We lucked out this week with the weather. I can't imagine being on the river with this lightning," I said.

The storm was fierce, but it didn't last long. Within an hour the rain had stopped, and the sun sporadically appeared between the thick clouds. Two of the other couples in our group arrived back at the cabin after the storm had passed. They had been on the Bright Angel Suspension Bridge when the rain started. They said they could feel the bridge swaying in the wind. Just before the rain started, Eric and crew passed under the bridge they were standing on. And then the skies opened. Not only were the people on the boats dealing with rain and lightning, but they also had a difficult rapid (Horn Creek) to run a couple of miles downstream. Not a great start to their trip.

With nothing else to do, most of the guys went and sat at the long tables in the canteen. It was open during the afternoon as a shelter for hikers, and more importantly, a place to have a beer. Craig, Phill, John and I claimed half of a table in the middle of the room and sat there leisurely drinking. "How's the ant bite, Phill?" I asked.

"Better. That sting relief stuff you gave me helped a lot, so did the cold water. I'm really surprised at how much that hurt," he replied.

That morning, Phill was in the latrine area and got stung on his leg by a red ant. It was a sting, but I called it a bite. He had been complaining about the pain all morning, which was unusual; he's not a complainer. When we'd arrived at Phantom Ranch, he pulled Eric aside and said, "Hey, I hate to even bother you with this, but I got stung by a red ant this morning, and it really hurts. I mean it *really* hurts. Do you have any suggestions for what I should do?" Eric advised running cold water on it. "If I were you, I'd put my leg in the creek over there. That's the best thing for it. As long as you're not allergic to the sting, you'll be fine."

I'd overheard their conversation and gave Phill a couple of

sting relief pads that I'd had in my pack for years, just in case of an emergency. They're topical anesthetic pads that dull the pain of a bite or sting. Phill applied them to the sting and then sat in the creek for a while. Apparently, that did the trick.

The canteen was only about a third full, but there was a constant flow of hikers in and out, buying snacks or beer, or checking into their room for the night. An older couple came in and sat at the other end of our table. (By older I mean older than me, which is getting to be a smaller group every day. I would guess they were in their late 60s.) They were sitting quietly drinking water, so we thought it would be courteous to strike up a conversation with them.

The husband did most of the talking. He told us that he had retired a few years before and that they love visiting the national parks, especially Grand Canyon. He and his wife had hiked down that morning and were spending the night in one of the cabins.

"Have you been here before?" I asked.

"Yes. We've been here to the ranch before. We love it here."

"Do you always hike, or do you sometimes take a mule?"

"Oh, we always hike. We don't move very fast, but we can get down and back to the top on our own."

"That's fantastic. Good for you. Do you visit other parks in the Southwest?" I asked.

"We do. We live in the Midwest and have a modified Fleetwood RV. We'll drive out west and spend a few weeks. We go to other places, but we keep coming back here."

"Well, I can see why. It's an amazing place."

"It sure is. This is the 62nd time my wife and I have hiked to Phantom Ranch."

"What, your 62nd time? Did I hear that correctly?"

"Yes. That's correct. This is our 62nd time down here."

We were speechless. For a moment I thought he was kidding us, but he wasn't. "You must have been coming here for years and years," I said.

"I think we first came here five years ago, maybe six."

"That means you've averaged once a month over that time."

"We take breaks, then we'll do it several times in a short spell depending on when we can catch cancellations here. We're coming back in a couple of weeks."

I didn't even know how to respond to what he was telling us. But still, good for them for getting out and doing a strenuous hike in one of the most beautiful places in the world. "So, do you always stay in a cabin when you come to Phantom Ranch?" I asked.

"We try. That's what we prefer. But if we have to, we'll sleep in the dorms. We don't camp," he replied. I was still reeling from what he told us about how many times they'd hiked to Phantom Ranch the past few years. Then he said, "I did a stupid thing today." He was rubbing the side of his hand while he was talking.

"Yeah, what was that?"

"We got into our cabin this morning; it was available when we arrived. I had put my pack on the bed, and I was standing there next to it. I saw something run across the bed, and I put my hand on it without thinking. That was stupid. I was trying to smash it, and it got me."

"What was it?" I asked

"A scorpion," he replied.

"Oh no, what did you do?"

"It hurt real bad, but I ran cold water on the sting right away, which helped. It still hurts though."

I was about to say, "If you think that's something, my friend Phill here got bit by an ant this morning. Show him, Phill." But I didn't get the chance. The wives walked through the front door of the canteen and were coming over to our table.

I said quickly, "Sir, our wives are coming over to sit with us. Please don't tell them your scorpion story. Please. Otherwise, we'll be hiking out of the Grand Canyon right now—with our thirty-pound duffel bags on our backs."

He laughed and nodded his head. The ladies sat down, and I looked at our new friend across the table and mouthed the words, "No scorpion." He laughed again.

A little bit later, when the manager of the canteen kicked us out so the staff could prepare the space for dinner, we all walked the thirty feet to our cabin and hung out in front. We recounted stories about our week and laughed. What a great trip it had been. In the midst of all of this, a tall young man with dark hair walked up and introduced himself. "Hey, everybody. I'm John. I'm your guide for the hike out tomorrow."

When they do a passenger exchange at Phantom Ranch, O.A.R.S. provides a guide who hikes with the new people coming down from the South Rim. The guide spends the night at Phantom Ranch, and then hikes back out the next day with the passengers leaving the trip. His job isn't complete until the last passenger makes it to the top of the South Rim. It's a park regulation that guided river trip groups have a "sweeper" to ensure everyone makes it to the top. John was our sweeper.

"We heard you had a long day today, John."

"Yeah, it took a little longer than normal, but everyone made it to the river."

We were pumping him for information about why it took some of the new passengers so long to hike down that morning, but he wouldn't tell us. "Some of the passengers had to take it slow, but that's OK. It also turned out to be a lot longer hike than I had planned on."

"Why? Did you not come down the Bright Angel Trail?"

"We did. However, I hiked a few extra miles. Part of my job is to stay at the back of the group and make sure everyone makes it to the river. Well, I was in the back with the last passengers when one of them realized they had left their glasses up on the rim. So, I offered to go back and get them."

"How far down were you when they figured this out?"

"We were about three and a half miles down."

"You hiked three and a half miles back up to get glasses? I would have told them they were out of luck."

"The passenger kept telling me not to go back, but I figured I had the time. They were moving slowly. That extra seven miles though made for a long hike."

"Yeah, I bet you're exhausted."

"I'm pretty tired, but I'll be fine."

At five o'clock the first dinner crowd gathered outside the canteen. Steak is served at the five o'clock seating, and that night there wasn't an unreserved seat to be had, which is typical. By six-thirty they had the first group fed, and the place cleared out ready for the rest of us, who had reservations for the second seating. The meal for the second session was Hiker's Stew. In addition to the stew, they served us salad, cornbread, and chocolate cake. Tea and water were on the table, and they also took orders for beer and wine.

The food was delicious and filling, but we missed the summer camp feel of the chair circle. Back at the cabin after dinner, I practiced packing the backpack I would carry out the next day. The pack was small, so I wanted to be sure it held all of the stuff I had planned to take with me. Everything else went into my duffel that the mule train would carry to the South Rim. "We need to take our bags to the duffel drop-off," I said to Karen. "I don't think we'll have time in the morning before we leave."

Outside behind the canteen was a table with a scale on it for weighing our bags. The weight limit was a strict thirty pounds per duffel, and the dimensions couldn't exceed thirty-six inches by twenty inches by thirteen inches. The instructions were to weigh your bag, place a strip of masking tape on the outside, and write your name and the weight of your bag on the tape. While we were trying to figure out how to use the scale, a ranger came by and helped us. We must have looked confused. The ranger didn't know that we always look that way.

"Where do we put our bags once they're weighed and tagged?" Karen asked the ranger.

"Just put them right here on top of these cages," she replied. There were several wooden shelves with doors on them that were locked. The doors had wooden frames and thick wire mesh faces. Inside we could see all of the other bags that were ready for the trip the next day.

"We just leave them here? Out in the open? Shouldn't they be locked up with the others?" Karen asked.

"They'll be alright there. One of the staff will come and put them away."

Back at the cabin, there was time enough to sit outside and finish the last of the whiskey we'd brought with us. This would be our last night together in the canyon. Tomorrow we would be back in civilization.

The group was worn out, and soon everyone headed for his or her cabin for bed. Phill and Wendy had their packs for the next day ready and sitting on their bunks. When they went to the restrooms to brush their teeth, it occurred to Craig and me that this was the perfect opportunity to put a large rock in Phill's pack. I found a softball-sized rock outside by the creek. We hurriedly emptied the pack, put the rock at the bottom, and carefully repacked everything. I tried to convince the wives to keep our secret, but they wouldn't commit. They were feeling sorry for Phill.

"This is how guys show their love for each other," I told Karen.

"Giving him a heart attack by tricking him into needlessly carrying a heavy pack up 5,000 feet?" she asked.

"Yes, exactly," I replied.

She just shook her head and went back to doing "fashion show" with her hiking outfit for the next day.

"By the way," she said without looking at us. "You put the rock in Wendy's pack."

Crap! We had to empty Wendy's pack, take the rock out, put everything back and then get the rock into Phill's pack before they got back from brushing their teeth. *We* almost had a heart attack.

"What did you think when you pulled women's clothes

out of what you thought was Phill's pack?" Karen asked.

I looked at Craig for an answer.

"Don't look at me," he said. "You didn't notice either."

"How much whiskey did you guys drink?" Karen asked.

I knew I wouldn't be able to keep a straight face when Phill and Wendy got back, so when they arrived, I immediately left for the restrooms to brush my teeth. Ten minutes later as I walked back, I heard, "I'm going to kill him!" coming from our cabin. Then, I heard everyone laughing. "Damn it," I thought. The women sold me out.

I opened the door to the cabin, and everyone was still laughing, but no one mentioned the rock. I picked up my pack, and of course, it was much heavier than it had been ten minutes earlier. I took the rock out of my pack and acted surprised that someone would play such a cruel trick on me.

I asked Phill, "Did Karen give me up?"

Phill said, "No, I figured it out on my own. But I gotta say, you almost got away with it. Had it been just a little lighter I wouldn't have suspected anything."

We pushed our luck. I should have chosen a smaller rock.

Now I had to worry about what Phill would do in retaliation. As the cabin lights went out for the night though, I was less concerned about Phill than I was about the scorpions. I kept thinking about the scorpion story our new friend told us that afternoon. I slept on top of the covers all night. That, I was sure, was a better plan than sleeping under the covers. Why this was a better plan, I didn't know, but that's what I did.

I didn't get much sleep that night. Between twitching and scratching every time I thought something brushed my leg and the fact that every person in the cabin including me got up at least once in the middle of the night to pee, I didn't sleep well. About 2:00 am I must have dozed off. Two hours later I was awake again. I had set the alarm clock in my head for 4:00 am.

Hanging out at Phantom Ranch. Left to right: Wendy (facing away), Iain, Joe, John, Craig, Bart, Aya, Gill, and Lolly.

The Phantom Ranch Canteen.

HIKING OUT

It was unanimous amongst the group that we'd get up at 4:30 am. Lights would be on, people would be bumping into each other, and there would be a semi-polite competition for the single bathroom in our little bunkhouse. This is why at 4:00 am I was wide-awake. I had placed my hiking clothes on my backpack at the foot of the bed. Before anyone else began stirring, I pulled the comforter on top of me and changed from my swim trunks—the last clean article of clothing I had when I took a shower the day before—into my hiking shorts and shirt. I was proud of myself for how quietly I was changing clothes and making it to the door of our cabin with my shaving kit, flip flops, and headlamp. That ended as I pulled the door open. It sounded like a cat getting its tail caught under a rocking chair. I quickly closed the door behind me and headed to the restroom/shower building that was about a hundred yards away.

I passed several people on my way, a surprising number I thought for the middle of the night. Hikers headed for the rim—north or south—get on the trail early to beat the heat.

There was no one in the men's bathroom while I washed up and brushed my teeth. I kept hearing a scraping and banging sound outside. I thought maybe someone was struggling with the door lock, but when I opened the door, there was no one there. When I finished my bathroom business, I gathered my stuff and walked back into the dark. My headlamp was lighting the path two feet in front of me; that's where I focused my attention as I headed toward the cabin. I heard a sound, and thinking it was someone walking toward me I looked up as I said, "Oh, excuse me." The deer I was now face-to-face with did not say, "excuse me," back.

He just stared at me motionless. Deer are not particularly frightening animals, although this one had large, pointy antlers and was less than an arm's length away. Being higher on the food chain than him, I expected him to scamper away immediately. He did not. He was probably expecting me to scamper back into the bathroom until he was finished grazing on the bushes growing against the side of the building. I realize that meeting a deer in the wilderness is not remarkable, but here's the thing: I couldn't get around him. The path we were on had thick vegetation on one side and the building on the other.

I didn't think it would be a good idea to try to shoo him away. If he didn't like my shooing, he could have easily given me a poke or two with his antlers. A minute or so later, another bathroom goer showed up and again, looking up at the very last moment found himself at the other end of the deer. The guy just stood there, blocking the deer's exit. I've heard wild animals don't like that. The three of us didn't move for a few minutes, which is a long time in a situation like this.

I kept giving the butt-end guy looks and nods, which he should have interpreted as "Back up!" but he didn't. Finally, I figured the only way out was to push through the thick vegetation and try to escape without getting too scraped up. As I began pushing the bushes aside the deer bolted, nearly knocking the other guy over. Then I had to use the bathroom again.

Back at the cabin I found, as I had expected I would, a bunch of half-asleep, grumpy people searching for their clothes and scratching themselves. Karen asked, "Where were you?" I explained my traumatic deer jam experience at the bathroom to which she replied, "That's it? You saw a deer? How terrifying! Are you OK? Did he try to nuzzle you?" I wanted to explain further that I was trapped and he could have poked me and, and, and, but by now the guys in the cabin were looking at me as if they were about to ask me to surrender my man card. The best thing to do in a situation like this is to divert attention. I said with a chuckle, "So, Phill, how's your backpack this morning?" He replied calmly, "Fine. How's yours?"

Hmmm, "I better dump everything out and check before hitting the trail," I thought.

As with dinner, Phantom Ranch had two seatings for breakfast, 5:00 am and 6:30 am. Reservations are required, and ours were for the early seating. There was a line of hikers at the canteen's door when they opened. Just like dinner, we ate family-style at long tables each with room for twelve people. Breakfast was more than enough: pancakes, biscuits, bacon, fruit, orange juice, and coffee. There wasn't much small talk at the table. People were mostly focused on getting fueled up and out of there. Afterward we each grabbed a sack lunch and headed back to the cabin for one last check for rocks in our backpacks.

One advantage we had on the hike out was we only had to carry the bare essentials in our packs since the mules would carry everything else. We only needed water, snacks, rain gear and a change of clothes; just enough to hike out and hold us over until we picked up our duffels at the mule barn later in the afternoon.

The weather was cool and cloudy that morning. A thick layer of clouds had replaced the thunderheads from the day before. Our previous hikes on Bright Angel Trail were in full sun and the temperatures were warm. Regardless, it's a strenuous ten-mile hike under any conditions.

We all met outside the canteen at 6:00 am. Once John, our hiking guide, made sure we were all accounted for, we began our single-file march toward the river. It was still dark and with our headlamps lit we looked like an early shift of miners reporting to work.

Karen and I started the hike in the middle of the pack. I must have been crowding the person in front of me because I could hear Karen behind me say, "It's not a race." The second time she said it her voice sounded much further away than the first time. I enjoy hiking fast. There is something satisfying about finding a level of heavy breathing that makes me feel as if I'm getting a good workout. When it's just the two of us hiking together I never leave Karen behind despite her dramatic, breathless pleas, "Go ahead, I'll meet you at the top." Then she usually coughs or wheezes loudly for added effect.

This hike was different: there were seventeen of us. We'd discussed this scenario before the trip. Karen told me many times, and I believed she was sincere, that it would be OK for me to go as fast as I'd like on the hike out. She wouldn't get eaten by a bear or lost. She even said, "I think I would enjoy hiking at a relaxed pace and being able to stop and take pictures whenever I want." Well, she got her chance, and when we discussed it afterward she said there were a couple of miles of the trail where she couldn't see anyone ahead of her or behind her. She loved that stretch because for about an hour she felt like she was the only person on the trail.

I took off and joined Bart and Joe at the front of the line. I knew Bart would be moving fast. He's in great shape and has long legs. Joe was with him step for step. It wasn't long before the three of us were a quarter of a mile ahead of the main group. We didn't talk much; we just kept moving forward at a good clip as the sky slowly brightened enough for us to turn our headlamps off.

I've heard the lecture many times: hiking quickly through the Grand Canyon is like running through a museum. Why would anyone do that? Well, we all enjoy the world around us differently. I was having a great time breathing hard and trying to keep up with Bart. It was a moving meditation, and I couldn't think of a better place in which to do it.

About two miles up the trail we passed the scorpion story guy and his wife. They were moving slowly. We said, "Hello," and, "Goodbye," without breaking stride. They must have started hiking way before we did to be that far ahead of us. It's inspiring to see people of all ages enjoying the parks and staying physically active.

The sun was beginning to hit the north rim of the canyon. The light was radiant so we stopped at a bend in the switchbacks and took a few photos. I kept taking photos, and then looking at my phone. The contrast of light and the incredible beauty of the landscape were impossible to capture.

As we started back up the trail, we saw a man running toward us holding a water bottle. Two more were in pouches wrapped around his waist. When he got close to us, he urgently yelled, "I'm running rim to rim" as if to let us know we needed to get out of his way. I thought that was odd. I wondered, "Does he plan on yelling that at every hiker he passes for the entire twenty-three miles?"

Hiking rim to rim has become a thing. People will start at one side of the canyon and hike to the other, often spending the night at Phantom Ranch at the bottom of the canyon. You can leave your car at one rim and take a shuttle service back once you get to the other side.

In my opinion, a civilized way to do a rim-to-rim hike is to park at the North Rim and spend the night at the lodge. Hike the next day the thirteen and a half miles to Phantom Ranch and spend the night. Then, the next day, hike the remaining nine and a half miles to the South Rim and spend the night at one of the lodges there. The next day take a shuttle back to the North Rim to pick up your car. You could also camp at each of those places instead of staying at the lodges. Hikers have told us they have also added overnight stops at Cottonwood Campground, between the North Rim and Phantom Ranch, and at Indian Garden, between Phantom Ranch and the South Rim.

Some people want more of a challenge. The runner who passed us was apparently attempting to run from rim to rim in a single day. I've heard hikers claim they have hiked rim to rim to rim with only short naps along the way. If you hang around the trail long enough someone will tell you they've gone from rim to rim to rim to rim without eating, sleeping or stopping.

The record for running from rim to rim is less than three hours—that's a distance of about twenty-three miles. It took Bart, Joe and I four hours to hike the nine and a half miles from Phantom Ranch to the South Rim, and I don't think I could have done it faster if a bear was chasing me.

It's great that everyone has his or her unique way of enjoying the park. The rim-to-rim runners don't bother anyone unless you're in their way when they're running downhill. The National Park Service may have a different opinion though. The rangers are the ones who have to respond to visitors who attempt these strenuous feats, and then need someone to rescue them. On the Grand Canyon National Park website is a warning, "Under no circumstances should you attempt to hike from the rim to the river and back in one day!" Exclamation point.

Halfway to the South Rim, we reached Indian Garden. On the hike up, this is the first place with toilets and water. There is also water available at both the three-mile and one and a half-mile rest stops. (The mileage designations of the rest stops are the distances from the trailhead at the South Rim.) At Indian Garden, we filled our water bottles and ate salty snacks. The National Park Service encourages hikers to eat salty snacks as well as drink plenty of water on strenuous hikes. Most people are familiar with the need to stay hydrated and the risks of dehydration. Fewer people know about the importance of having enough salt.

Low blood sodium (hyponatremia) can cause symptoms such as fatigue, headache, nausea, muscle cramps, confusion, and irritability. Hikers sometimes confuse these symptoms as signs of dehydration, but drinking more water without taking in sodium can make the problem worse. So, at Indian Garden, I broke out my bag of salted peanuts and had a snack.

Joe insisted we rest for five minutes, but Bart never sat down or stopped pacing. A few moments later he started wandering up the trail. Joe and I knew if we didn't follow we wouldn't see him again until the top. As we got within sight of the three-mile hut, she began lobbying for another rest. "Three minutes. We can sit down and rest for three minutes." We stopped for a bathroom break and sat on the stone ledge by the trail. Bart even sat this time, saying, "Yeah, we don't need to go so fast. I have this competitive streak in me when I'm doing outdoor activities. It just happens."

As we were sitting there, we looked downhill trying to spot the rest of the group. We couldn't see them, but I thought this would be a good time to tease Bart about his competitiveness. I said, "Wait, is that Phil? I think he's trying to catch us." I was joking of course. I smiled and looked at Joe, who rolled her eyes and said, "Why did you have to say that?" I looked over at Bart, and he was gone. He had started up the trail.

It took all of our energy to keep up with him. At the one and a half-mile water spigot, Bart slowed down enough for Joe and me to catch him. She said, "One minute. Let's rest for one minute." We didn't stop and rest, but we slowed down long enough for Joe to fill her water bottle. I was getting light-headed and trying to stay with Bart while I ate the last of my peanuts. Once he sped up again, I did too. By now Joe was a fading figure behind us. I could hear her doing the best Karen impression she could muster, "One minute. Just, one, minute, [loud wheeze]." Then she was gone, and we were picking up speed. I could no longer stay right behind Bart. My new goal was to be able to still see him when he reached the very top. That goal didn't last very long. Now *I* was by myself.

At a quarter of a mile from the top, I hit a wall. I was concerned I wouldn't make it the rest of the way. The final stretch was a serious challenge. I wasn't thinking clearly. I may have stumbled backward a few times. There was a moment when I thought I heard Phill behind me ask with a chuckle, "How's your backpack, Matt?" I looked behind me, but Phill wasn't there.

I was out of water. I was out of salty snacks. I was wet, cold and very much had to pee. Joe passed me then she faded out of sight. Despite my consciousness leaving my body and floating above me for the last hundred yards, I made it to the top under my own power. Bart and Joe were there. They had been looking over the edge to make sure I made it.

We exchanged weary high-fives. Joe was back to her energetic, cheery self as if the hike never happened. I would need the rest of the day to recover. At that moment though, I was in dire need of a restroom visit. I skipped the congratulatory small talk and took off. I didn't know where the public restrooms were, but I figured that I was likely to find one in either direction. I was correct. By the bus stop west of the Bright Angel cabins, there was a brand new complex of restrooms, each one a separate room measuring about eight feet by ten feet.

Normally I'm not a big fan of the toilet huts in the national parks. I'd rather go behind my car in the parking lot while no one is looking or hold it for a couple of days than breathe in one of those places. This one, though, seemed luxurious. It was spacious. It was warm. It smelled better than me. I thought, "I'm a good half an hour ahead of Karen, I might take a nap in here while I wait." It had a door with a working doorknob and lock, a roof, a toilet that flushed, and a sink. What else would you need? The thought went through my mind, "I could live in here. There might even be room for Karen. The floor's a little wet, but we can fix that." This is yet another benefit of spending time in the wilderness: your awareness and appreciation of things completely resets.

It didn't take long for the rest of our group to make it to the top of the canyon. While we were hiking, it seemed as if there was a lot of distance between us, but time wise, there wasn't more than a half an hour difference between the first and last of our group.

I was walking back to the trailhead just as the last six hikers made it to the top with John, our guide, right behind them. When John got to the end of the trail he started running: no high-fives, no goodbyes, no thank yous, he just took off. I thought that was odd; he seemed like such a personable guy. Later I found out that when he had reached Indian Garden on the hike up, John's phone connected to cell service for the first time in about twenty-two hours. That's when he learned that his pregnant wife was in labor.

When the group he was hiking with heard this, they encouraged him to run ahead so he could get to his wife more quickly, but he refused. It was his job to see everyone to the top, and he was insistent that he finish the job. From that point forward, the group picked up the pace so John could get out of there as quickly as possible.

Lolly and John at the top of Bright Angel Trail.

Happy to be at the top. Left to right: Aya, Craig, Iain, Paul, Debi, and Gill.

SOUTH RIM

All of the couples in our group had reserved rooms at the El Tovar Hotel for the night, rather than taking a shuttle back to Flagstaff that day. We'd all made it to the rim by about 11:00 am; too early to check into our rooms. Some of us went to the bar at El Tovar for an early lunch. The mood of the group was part celebratory that we survived the hike out of the canyon and part sad that the trip was over.

When it came time to pay the bill for lunch, I reached for my wallet and knew something was wrong. "Where's my wallet?" I thought. It took me a second to remember that I didn't bring my wallet on the trip, but I did take my driver's license, credit card and $100 cash with me in case I needed them at Phantom Ranch. I remembered I had them in the shorts (my swim trunks to be exact) I was wearing the day before. I started to wonder what I had done with those shorts when I changed out of them that morning.

Then it hit me. Out of fear of being trapped under the covers with a scorpion, I had slept on top of them in my clothes the night before. When I woke up, I changed into my hiking clothes while lying on the bed. To keep Wendy, who was sleeping in the bunk closest to me, from seeing me naked—and I know she was looking my way while pretending to be asleep—I pulled the top cover over myself and changed underneath it. In my haste to get up, I had left my shorts between the covers. That's where my driver's license, credit card, and cash were: in my shorts, in the bed, under the covers, way down at the bottom of the canyon.

"You can't be serious," Karen said when I explained to her what happened.

"Yes. I'm serious. It's Wendy's fault," I replied.

Wendy, who was with us at lunch, snickered and said, "You wish."

With little energy to do anything else, the group took turns making fun of me and then giving me suggestions on how to remedy my predicament—none of which were helpful. I told Karen she would have to pay for lunch, "Well, that's not going to happen for at least three hours," she replied. "My credit card is in my duffel bag, which is on the back of a mule right about now.

John interrupted, "Hey everybody, the Smiths are doing the 'we forgot our credit card' thing again. It looks like I'll be paying for all of us, again."

Leaving my valuable stuff at the bottom of the canyon wasn't my only mistake. Aya interrupted the group while they were giving me trouble to ask, "Wait. Why were you sleeping on top of the covers?" She had also slept in the same cabin the night before.

I looked at Craig for help. He said, "Well you can tell her now, we're no longer down there."

"I was afraid there might be a scorpion between the covers of my bed," I said.

She gave me an odd look and asked, "Why were you afraid there might be a scorpion in your bed?"

I looked at Craig again. He said, "You're in too deep now."

I told her the story about the man we'd met in the canteen and how he had been stung by a scorpion the day before in the cabin just down the path from our cabin. All of the wives were leaning in as I told the story. The table erupted when I got to the part about the scorpion running across the bed.

"When were you going to tell us?"

"And you let us sleep in that cabin?"

"What else did he tell you?"

"I can't believe you didn't say anything to us!"

"What if one of us had gotten stung?"

I let them vent for a while and then said, "Don't blame me. These guys all knew, and they didn't say anything either."

Karen came to my defense, "I'm glad you didn't tell us. I would *not* have slept a wink if I knew there might be scorpions in our cabin."

"Thank you," I said to her. "See, I was doing you a favor," I said in the direction of the other wives. "Now, I have to get back to my emergency. I've lost my shorts."

For the next couple of hours, I thought about canceling my credit card, calling it a loss, and letting Karen do the driving back to Seattle. "Let's just go to the Bright Angel Lodge and talk to the person at the desk who handles the Phantom Ranch reservations. Maybe they can find your shorts," Karen suggested.

"So you think we can go to the reservation desk, have them call down to the ranch, ask them to find my shorts, have them check to make sure the credit card, driver's license and money are still in them, and then have a mule bring them back up here to the rim tomorrow—that's your plan?" I asked in a skeptical tone.

"It's worth a try," she replied.

I went with Karen to the Bright Angel Lodge more because I had nothing else to do than because I thought her plan would work. Ten minutes later the friendly gentleman at the reservation desk hung up the phone said to me, "They have your shorts, and the credit card and cash are still in them. They'll be at the mule barn across the street tomorrow at about 1:00 pm. You can pick 'em up then." Sweet! Except our shuttle back to Flagstaff was leaving the next day at 10:00 am. We'd have to take the shuttle to Flagstaff, pick up our truck, and drive right back to the South Rim to pick up my shorts. That would be a hassle, but better than having to cancel and replace the card and get a new driver's license.

Karen and I spent part of the afternoon poking around Hopi House across the parking lot from the El Tovar. Hopi House looks like an ancient adobe pueblo, but it was designed by Mary Colter and built in 1904. For over a hundred years it's been a gift shop with a wide selection of authentic Native American art.

We were still acclimating to the hordes of people as we walked to the main Visitor Center along the rim trail. The crowds on the South Rim were overwhelming in contrast to what we'd become used to during our week on the river. The South Rim is the most visited area of the park. It's great that so many people want to see the canyon, but being in such close contact with that many tourists makes me cranky. In the course of about thirty yards I was coughed on, sneezed on, and someone spit right at my feet. I turned toward Karen to suggest we go back to the hotel when she hollered, "Look out!" grabbed me by the arm, and pulled me close to her. A family had been walking past us with a very large dog. One of the kids was tossing a bag full of dog poop in the air, and it would have hit me in the face if Karen hadn't saved me.

"Jacob! Why are you throwing that bag in the air? You almost hit that man with it. Stop that right now!" the mom said.

Without looking in my direction, Jacob yelled, "Sorry!" and then chased his little sister to the edge of the rim by swinging the bag of poop at her.

"Jacob!" his mom cried as she tried to keep the kids from plunging over the side.

In addition to the crowds milling about, there were people taking selfies on the edge of the canyon. It always makes me uncomfortable when I walk along the rim and see so many people standing inches from a sheer drop-off, especially when there are several in a group looking at the camera rather than where they're placing their feet. Karen asked a ranger once if people are allowed to be way out on the edge. "There's no rule against it," she said. "We allow visitors to go where they want. We try to warn them, but accidents happen."

Lightning in the distance over the canyon forced us to abandon our walk to the Visitor Center. We high-tailed it back to the El Tovar before the downpour started. Rain drenched the rim and sent the visitors scurrying for cover. Fortunately for us, some of the members of our group had pulled a couple of tables together in the hotel's bar area and claimed a few extra chairs before they were all taken. We sat there, had a beer and watched it rain.

While we drank and chatted, I could already feel the group pulling apart, not in an unkind way, but we were all once again connected to the outside world through our phones and distracted by electronic messages or the thought of what we would be doing tomorrow or the next day many miles away. The benefit of being disconnected and basically trapped in the wilderness for a week was that it caused us to be present with each other. That's what I was feeling slip away.

Eventually, the rain stopped and the crowds returned to the rim. I began to notice people in the bar craning their necks to look out the windows that face the rim of the canyon, and then walking outside quickly. One of the bartenders was looking toward the canyon when she said, "Wow, we don't see that very often." Outside, over the canyon, were spectacular rainbows. I grabbed my phone and followed the masses to the edge of the overlook.

The storm that had brought the torrential rains was now giving us a fantastic light show. To the east of the canyon, a streak of light that looked like a vertical band of fire stretched from the clouds down to a plateau just beyond the horizon. Behind the streak, the clouds glowed with orange light.

Storms had bookended our trip. Looking at the downpours off in the distance we felt fortunate that the rain held off while we were on the river. At the same time, we were hoping that the new group of river travelers was having a safe start to their journey.

View of the Grand Canyon from the South Rim, rainbows in the distance.

Matt on the South Rim of the Grand Canyon

GOING HOME

The sky the next morning was clear as a bell and the colors of the canyon were vivid due to the rain from the previous day. Standing in the lobby of the El Tovar Hotel, waiting for our shuttle, our group was unrecognizable from the photo we'd taken on our last morning on the river. Showered, shampooed and shaved: the grubbiness was gone.

The ride back to Flagstaff went off without a hitch. We all exchanged hurried goodbyes with our fellow travelers as everyone headed somewhere in a rush. Karen and I had a long road in front of us and not much time to get home. Our daughter's birthday was the next day, and we never miss our kids' birthdays, no matter how old they are. The drive would take us twenty-one hours. We gathered our luggage from the storage locker at the DoubleTree, got in our truck and started back toward the South Rim.

I was hoping the mules had made good time that morning coming up the canyon, so I went to the Phantom Ranch desk at Bright Angel Lodge as soon as we got there to see if they knew when I could pick up my package at the barn. "Oh, I'm sorry, sir. The rains yesterday washed out part of the trail, and the mules are having a hard time making it back. Why don't you try stopping by the barn around 3:00 pm. Hopefully, they'll be there by then." My shoulders dropped, and I gave

Karen an exasperated look. There's only one thing to do when faced with a frustrating situation like this: drink beer and eat pizza.

We walked to the Maswik Lodge and fortunately got a table in their pizza parlor right before the lunch crowd arrived. Karen and I tried our best to eat slowly and relax; we still had at least a couple of hours to wait. While we were in the restaurant, Lolly texted Karen. She and John had stopped by the O.A.R.S. warehouse in Flagstaff hoping to see the *Emerald Mile*, the dory for which the book is named. It's hanging in O.A.R.S.' facility. Lolly had taken a few great photos of the famous boat and sent them to Karen. The images made us want to be back on the river.

By 2:30 pm, we'd walked along the rim, stopped in every gift shop and studio, and were more than ready to get on the road. We decided to go to the barn and wait for the mules to arrive. Thankfully, when we got there, the staff was unloading them from their trailers. I found the head mule-wrangler and asked him if he had a special delivery for Matt Smith. "A what?" he asked with a confused expression on his face. "I don't have any special delivery. If you're waiting for your duffel, they'll put it in the barn over there."

"No, it's not a duffel. The folks down at the ranch were supposed to send up a swimming suit with today's mule train," I replied.

"A what?"

"A swimming suit."

"A what?"

I was about to say the heck with it and head back to my truck when I tried one more time. "Are you sure they didn't send a small package up the trail this morning with the mules? It had my driver's license and a credit card in it."

"Well, I don't know. They did give me this." He reached into the cab of his truck and pulled out a clear plastic bag with "Matt Smith" written in large letters on the side in black magic marker. My swimming suit was inside the bag.

"Yes! That's it! Thank you." I pulled the swimming suit

out of the bag, and inside the back pocket were my credit card, driver's license, and five twenty-dollar bills. Thank you, Phantom Ranch!

He said with a smile "You're certainly welcome. Now, you have a nice day." I think he had been messing with me. I probably would have done the same thing.

Karen and I rushed back to the truck, weaving our way through the crowds of visitors. As we drove east out of the park, we didn't talk much; we were both thinking about our time on the river. I was remembering the last time I saw the dories and the crew...

After we had disembarked at Phantom Ranch and cleaned up, Karen and I walked to the Bright Angel Suspension Bridge. Halfway across the bridge, we stopped for a while and gazed downriver. We missed it already.

At the far side of the bridge we took the trail that led to the Kaibab Suspension Bridge, intending to make a loop back to Phantom Ranch. Between the bridges, we ran into four other couples in our group, and together we hiked onto the Kaibab Suspension Bridge. From up there, we could easily see the boat beach; the dories and support rafts were still there. It looked like all of the new passengers had arrived and Eric was taking them through a safety orientation. It was odd seeing strangers sitting in *our* dories.

The ten of us stood on the bridge looking down at the scene below when thunder from the approaching storm rumbled through the canyon. As we turned to go, Bart said, "Wait, I have an idea." He told us his plan, and we all nodded in agreement. When we were ready, he cupped his hands around his mouth, took a deep breath, and yelled, "Dories!" The rest of us yelled, "Ho!" The canyon walls seemed to magnify our voices. Everyone on the beach looked up at us. The boatmen and crew smiled and gave us lingering waves. It was our final goodbye.

The End

Left to right: Mark, Rachel, Debi, Paul, Joe, Bart, Aya, Craig, Gill, Iain, Wendy (kneeling), Karen, Matt, Lolly, John, and Phill.

Left to right: JB, B, Andrew, Betsy, Andy, Maia, Q, Andre, Eric (sitting), Rondo

ABOUT THE AUTHORS

Matt and Karen have been married for over thirty-four years and live in the Seattle, Washington area. They have three adult children: Rachel, Emily and Matthew. Rachel and her husband Justin have two children of their own: Hadley and Clara. Having both grown up in the Midwest, Matt and Karen met at the University of Kansas and have been together ever since. *Dories, Ho!* is their second book project together. Their first book, also a travel memoir, is titled *Dear Bob and Sue.*

HOW TO CONTACT US

Email us at mattandkarensmith@gmail.com
or visit our website at www.mattandkaren.com

OTHER WORKS BY MATT AND KAREN

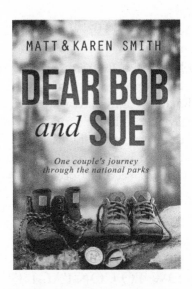

Dear Bob and Sue is the story of our journey to all fifty-nine U.S. National Parks. We wrote the book as a series of emails to our friends, Bob and Sue, in which we share our humorous and quirky observations. It is at times irreverent, unpredictable and sarcastic, all in the spirit of humor. We describe a few of our experiences in each park but do not provide an exhaustive overview of each experience or park. We didn't intend for this book to be a travel guide nor a recommendation for how to visit all fifty-nine of the U.S. National Parks although many readers have said they've found it to be a useful guide. Rather, it is our story about how we did it.

If you enjoy quirky humor set in the magnificent U.S. National Parks, this book may be for you. If you are looking for eloquent descriptions of the natural beauty we encountered or detailed descriptions of every activity you can do in each park, there are many other books available where you can find that information. All that said, many readers have commented that it's "laugh out loud" funny and a light-hearted glimpse of our journey through the parks.